CLASSIC SPIRITUALITY FOR THE MODERN MAN

Andrew Lynn has a Ph.D. in Renaissance literature from Cambridge University. He now works to help resolve international and cross-border disputes.

www.andrewlynn.com

CLASSIC SPIRITUALITY FOR THE MODERN MAN

Andrew Lynn

Howgill House Books

www.howgillhousebooks.com

Copyright © Andrew Lynn 2017

ISBN 978-1-912360-05-5

CONTENTS

INTRODUCTION

Hard times create strong men. Strong men create good times. Good times create weak men. Weak men create hard times.

The basic premise of this book is that strength and weakness have a spiritual dimension.

It is a man's awareness that he partakes in a higher order of reality that gives him the backbone and fortitude to withstand the many challenges he will encounter in life. Once a man appreciates, however dimly, that he is one aspect or manifestation of the transcendent source of being, then he begins to appreciate his own intrinsic dignity. And once a man begins to appreciate his own intrinsic dignity, everything changes for him.

The transformation occurs on several levels.

It begins on the personal level. If we all partake, in some mysterious way, of the divine, then we naturally start to treat ourselves with more respect: that means to bring under control damaging impulsivity and to commit to healthy physical, mental, and emotional development. This spreads out into our communities, because it goes without saying that if one person—by virtue of their humanity—partakes of the divine, so does the next person, and the next person after that, and the respect due to ourselves we will also find to be due to others. Finally, the transformation manifests on the political level, for tyrannical governments work through carrot and stick—and what cares a man for carrot and stick when he knows that has an infinite source of carrots and that no stick can really hurt him?

So why is it that young men, in the West at least, generally show little interest in spirituality?

It is undoubtedly true that mainstream religions have often found difficulty communicating their value effectively in the modern age. Modern Christianity has tended to present to the world a mixture of apathetic moralism, seemingly with the primary goal of causing minimum offence, coupled with an anodyne metaphysics that fails to reflect the subtlety and diversity of its own historic traditions. Islam suffers from the opposite difficulty: to outsiders it can be perceived, wrongly no doubt, as harsh, unforgiving, and unwelcoming. The Far Eastern faiths have done better at appealing to modern concerns but sometimes at the cost of sacrificing their complexity: there are only so many times that one can remain 'mindful' or 'live in the present' without asking if this is a sufficient way to address man's basic condition.

Exacerbating these internal weaknesses are

powerful political and economic forces arrayed against any resurgence in spiritual consciousness. These are forces that have been successful, on the whole, in breaking down traditional values and denigrating historic achievements. For them, nothing could be more undesirable than the reawakening of the diverse nations of the world to full consciousness of their intrinsic dignity and strength.

There's nothing 'conservative', then, about the brand of spiritual teaching that you will find in this book. It has famously been said that, in a time of universal deceit, telling the truth is a revolutionary act. We could equally well say that, in a time of universal triviality, seeking answers to the great questions of existence is likewise a revolutionary course of action. It is those who have unthinkingly adopted the self-satisfied assumptions and prejudices of their own era—including the presupposition that the search for the answers to the deep questions of existence, a search conducted by virtually all societies prior to around the mid-twentieth century, is an exercise in futility—who are the real conservatives. Those who have the humility to ask the question 'Could it be *us* who have gone astray?' are the true radicals, for it is they who are willing to challenge the complacency of the present age.

There is a kind of militant atheism afoot that purports to show that faith is incompatible with science and that people do awful things in the name of religion. It's true, of course, that we can't prove the existence of a supreme being or higher power. But it was also true that cavemen in their day would have been unable to prove the existence of electricity or radio waves—if they had even known that such things existed. As for the bad things people do in the name of religion, it should be obvious that people have done bad things in the name of politics and science too, but we would never give up on trying to establish better societies or to better understand the universe in which we find ourselves.

'Spirituality' for the purposes of this book is best defined as a visceral engagement with the deep questions of existence. *Visceral*, because you've got to feel it in your marrow and through your whole being. *Engagement*, because it happens when life grabs you by the collar and roughs you up a bit, forcing you to take notice. And *questions*, because we are not able to give answers until the slow process of awakening has reached its end—and sometimes not even then. Spirituality in this sense is always empowering even if not always comfortable. It is an implacable enemy of smallness.

We begin with *The Kybalion*, a work that summarizes the fundamental principles of spiritual wisdom—the principles of correspondence and polarity, for example—said to have been transmitted from as far back as ancient Egypt. From there we move on to *Ecclesiastes* of the Hebrew Bible—a work that in its brutal honesty and practical wisdom is unlike anything you may have come across elsewhere.

Our next stop is ancient China and the *Tao Te Ching* of Lao-tzu, a Daoist classic that teaches of the mysterious force that runs through all things and how to bring our being into harmony with it. Two works from the Buddhist tradition follow: the *Dhammapada*, which lays out wise guidance for living well, and the *Vitakkasanthana Sutta*, or 'On Governance of Thoughts', a precise guide to maintaining mental and emotional equilibrium. We return to Daoism in *The Writings of Chuang-tzu*, where we are instructed in the art of self-realisation, before turning to the *Bhagavad Gita* which expounds—by reference to dharma, yoga, and war—a spiritual path that is bold, brave, noble, and active. Bringing to an end the first half of the book are the works of two Sufi masters, al-Ghazali's *The Alchemy of Happiness* and Rumi's *The Masnavi*, which teach the cultivation of self as an agent of the divine.

Modern spiritual classics are the focus of the second half of the book. Blaise Pascal begins this part with his famous wager: it is quite logical, he shows using an early version of game theory, to believe in God. Two Germans come next: Arthur Schopenhauer, in 'On the Vanity of Existence', opens the way for a spiritual path in an atheistic age, whereas Friedrich Nietzsche, in *Thus Spoke Zarathustra*, points to a form of transcendence that can be achieved by calling upon the unrecognized potential of our nature. We conclude with James Allen's *As a Man Thinketh*, which brings us full circle back to the age-old principle that the process of renewal and transformation, which is at the heart of all true spirituality, must start from within.

One of the most spiritually aware men of the last century, CS Lewis, made a prediction. There would begin to appear, dotted here and there all over the earth, he said, a new kind of man. They will not much resemble your ideas of 'religious people' and they will not draw attention to themselves. But they will have voices and faces different from ours—stronger, quieter, happier, and more radiant. They will appear to have a lot of time—so much so that you will wonder where it comes from. You will tend to think you are being kind to them when they are being kind to you; they will love you more than other men—and need you less.

The 'new man' that this book seeks to inspire will be informed by the wisdom of many eras and several faiths. Many of the texts embody what has been called the 'perennial philosophy'—the universal core of spiritual wisdom that is found within all major traditions—but they have not been selected in order to convince you of anything. They have been chosen for one reason and one reason alone: individually—and, still more, collectively—they have the capacity to open you up to new dimensions of being, awareness, and strength. For millennia, your forebears viewed these matters as being of the utmost importance. It is, of course, your right to turn away from them if you wish. But if you are willing to entertain the possibility that generations of men have not been fantasists and fools, then read on. There is no time in history when man has needed this input more than he does today.

THE KYBALION

INTRODUCTION

There's really nothing quite like *The Kybalion*.

The work claims to be the distillation of ancient wisdom from as far back as Egypt of the pharaohs. It was there, so we are told, that the 'masters' first gathered together a store of timeless knowledge about the workings of the universe. Among those masters was a 'master of masters' known as Hermes Trismegistus—Hermes the 'thrice-great'. The details of his life have been lost. What remains is the legend: he was deified first by the Egyptians themselves (as Thoth, god of writing, magic, and wisdom) and then by the ancient Greeks (as Hermes, messenger of the gods). Thereafter he gave his name to Hermeticism—a body of writings believed by its adherents to constitute the single true theology, present in all religions, which had been given by God to man in antiquity.

The teachings associated with Hermes have for centuries informed the Western world's understanding of man's role in the cosmos. Hermes was known in the classical world of ancient Greece and Rome. Several Christian writers—from Augustine to Pico della Mirandola—considered him to be a wise pagan portending the arrival of Christianity. Isaac Newton studied the *Corpus Hermeticum*, the ancient writings attributed to Hermes, in detail. It has even been suggested that Hermes has a role to play in the Islamic tradition, appearing in the Koran as the prophet Idris.

Hermeticism has, nevertheless, for most of its long history been a secret wisdom. There are at least two reasons for that. In the first place, its practitioners intended their knowledge to be made available only to those capable of appreciating it—it was undesirable, so they considered, to 'cast pearls before swine'. But also it was necessary to avoid persecution from those who opposed the teachings: in the Middle Ages, that meant the Christians who fought the doctrine 'with fire and sword; stake, gibbet and cross'; during the Enlightenment, it meant the champions of the new mechanistic science. Hermeticism was, accordingly, transmitted to its disciples by way of terse maxims (such as, famously, 'as above, so below') and metaphors (such as the metaphor of alchemy) the true meaning of which would remain hidden to the uninitiated. To this day, the word 'hermetic' is used to refer to secret or tightly sealed matters.

The Kybalion itself is shrouded in mystery. Originally published in 1908, it is said to have been written by 'Three Initiates' who have chosen to remain anonymous. We have no way of knowing for certain from where its contents have come.

For the purposes of this book, however, that doesn't matter. What matters is that *The Kybalion* explains, in language that can be understood by all, the core elements of what is perhaps the most profound and enduring of the Western spiritual traditions. It does that by identifying and describing the seven principles of Hermetic wisdom: the principle of mentalism, the principle of correspondence, the principle of vibration, the principle of polarity, the principle of rhythm, the principle of cause and effect, and the principle of gender. Each principle is introduced by a pithy maxim or axiom, which is next elucidated in greater detail. Each of the principles is then given a chapter of its own.

It isn't surprising that the principle of mentalism comes first, as it is this that underpins the whole philosophy. The Kybalion says that 'All is mind'. The 'All' here refers to the substantial reality underlying all its manifestations. If the All is mind, all things arising out of that All are, to some degree, aspects of that universal mind. The universal mind is immanent within us much like playwrights and novelists are immanent within the characters they have created. As aspects or manifestations of that universal mind, we are able to act within and upon it accordingly; we are not, as some of the philosophers might have it, isolated minds confronting an alien and unresponsive physical world.

The Kybalion provides simple principles with far-reaching implications. To think in terms of polarity, for instance, is to appreciate the essential continuity of phenomena: heat and cold are really the same thing, being different in degree not in kind, just as love and hate are extremes having more in common with each other than either do with indifference. To think in terms of rhythm is to accept the inevitable to-and-fro of existence, and comprehend why pushing hard in one direction eventually generates counter-momentum in the other. To think in terms of cause and effect is to know that every thought we think, and every act we perform, will have both direct and indirect results, and that 'chance' is simply a word used to describe causation that is not yet understood.

The Hermetic teachings have unique attractions for the modern man. They are the West's particular contribution to the spiritual traditions of the world and their fundamental principles remain as fresh and relevant as at any time in history. Where mainstream or orthodox religion tends to demand self-abnegation, this is a path that offers knowledge, insight, and self-development. That alone should render it worthy of your consideration.

CHAPTER II

THE SEVEN HERMETIC PRINCIPLES

'The principles of truth are seven; he who knows these, understandingly, possesses the magic key before whose touch all the doors of the temple fly open.'—The Kybalion.

The seven Hermetic principles, upon which the entire Hermetic philosophy is based, are as follows:

1. The Principle of Mentalism.
2. The Principle of Correspondence.
3. The Principle of Vibration.
4. The Principle of Polarity.
5. The Principle of Rhythm.
6. The Principle of Cause and Effect.
7. The Principle of Gender.

These seven principles will be discussed and explained as we proceed with these lessons. A short explanation of each, however, may as well be given at this point.

13

1. THE PRINCIPLE OF MENTALISM

'The All is mind; The universe is mental.'—The Kybalion.

This principle embodies the truth that 'all is mind'. It explains that the All (which is the substantial reality underlying all the outward manifestations and appearances which we know under the terms of 'the material universe'; the 'phenomena of life'; 'matter'; 'energy'; and, in short, all that is apparent to our material senses) is spirit which in itself is unknowable and undefinable, but which may be considered and thought of as a universal, infinite, living mind. It also explains that all the phenomenal world or universe is simply a mental creation of the All, subject to the laws of created things, and that the universe, as a whole, and in its parts or units, has its existence in the mind of the All, in which mind we 'live and move and have our being'. This principle, by establishing the mental nature of the universe, easily explains all of the varied mental and psychic phenomena that occupy such a large portion of the public attention, and which, without such explanation, are non-understandable and defy scientific treatment. An understanding of this great Hermetic principle of mentalism enables the individual to readily grasp the laws of the mental universe, and to apply the same to his well-being and advancement. The Hermetic student is enabled to apply intelligently the great mental laws, instead of using them in a haphazard manner. With the master-key in his possession, the student may unlock the many doors of the mental and psychic temple of knowledge, and enter the same freely and intelligently. This principle explains the true nature of 'energy', 'power', and 'matter', and why and how all these are subordinate to the mastery of mind. One of the old Hermetic masters wrote, long ages ago: 'He who grasps the truth of the mental nature of the universe is well advanced on the path to mastery.' And these words are as true today as at the time they were first written. Without this master-key, mastery is impossible, and the student knocks in vain at the many doors of the temple.

2. THE PRINCIPLE OF CORRESPONDENCE

'As above, so below; as below, so above.'—The Kybalion.

This principle embodies the truth that there is always a correspondence between the laws and phenomena of the various planes of being and life. The old Hermetic axiom ran in these words: 'As above, so below; as below, so above.' And the grasping of this principle gives one the means of solving many a dark paradox, and hidden secret of nature. There are planes beyond our knowing, but when we apply the principle of correspondence to them we are able to understand much that would otherwise be unknowable to us. This principle is of universal application and manifestation, on the various planes of the material, mental, and spiritual universe—it is a universal law. The ancient Hermetists considered this principle as one of the most important mental instruments by which man was able to pry aside the obstacles which hid from view the unknown. Its use even tore aside the veil of Isis to the extent that a glimpse of the face of the goddess might be caught. Just as a knowledge of the principles of geometry enables man to measure distant suns and their movements, while seated in his observatory, so a knowledge of the principle of correspondence enables man to reason intelligently from the known to the unknown. Studying the monad, he understands the archangel.

3. THE PRINCIPLE OF VIBRATION

'Nothing rests; everything moves; everything vibrates.'—The Kybalion.

This principle embodies the truth that 'everything is in motion'; 'everything vibrates'; 'nothing is at rest'; facts which modern science endorses, and which each new scientific discovery tends to verify. And yet this Hermetic principle was enunciated thousands of years ago, by the masters of ancient Egypt. This principle explains that the differences between different manifestations of matter, energy, mind, and even spirit, result largely from varying rates of vibration. From the All, which is pure spirit, down to the grossest form of matter, all is in vibration—the higher the vibration, the higher the position in the scale. The vibration of spirit is at such an infinite rate of intensity and rapidity that it is practically at rest—just as a rapidly moving wheel seems to be motionless. And at the other end of the scale, there are gross forms of matter whose vibrations are so low as to seem at rest. Between these poles, there are millions upon millions of varying degrees of vibration. From corpuscle and electron, atom and molecule, to worlds and universes, everything is in vibratory motion. This is also true on the planes of energy and force (which are but varying degrees of vibration); and also on the mental planes (whose states depend upon vibrations); and even on to the spiritual planes. An understanding of this principle, with the appropriate formulas, enables Hermetic students to control their own mental vibrations as well as those of others. The masters also apply this principle to the conquering of natural phenomena, in various ways. 'He who understands the Principle of Vibration, has grasped the scepter of power,' says one of the old writers.

4. THE PRINCIPLE OF POLARITY

'Everything is dual; everything has poles; everything has its pair of opposites; like and unlike are the same;

*opposites are identical in nature, but different in
degree; extremes meet; all truths are but half-truths;
all paradoxes may be reconciled.'—The Kybalion.*

This principle embodies the truth that 'everything is
dual'; 'everything has two poles'; 'everything has its
pair of opposites', all of which were old Hermetic
axioms. It explains the old paradoxes, that have
perplexed so many, which have been stated as
follows: 'thesis and antithesis are identical in nature,
but different in degree'; 'opposites are the same,
differing only in degree'; 'the pairs of opposites may
be reconciled'; 'extremes meet'; 'everything is and
isn't, at the same time'; 'all truths are but half-truths';
'every truth is half-false'; 'there are two sides to
everything', etc., etc., etc. It explains that in
everything there are two poles, or opposite aspects,
and that 'opposites' are really only the two extremes
of the same thing, with many varying degrees
between them. To illustrate: heat and cold, although
'opposites', are really the same thing, the differences
consisting merely of degrees of the same thing. Look
at your thermometer and see if you can discover
where 'heat' terminates and 'cold' begins! There is no
such thing as 'absolute heat' or 'absolute cold'—the
two terms 'heat' and 'cold' simply indicate varying
degrees of the same thing, and that 'same thing'
which manifests as 'heat' and 'cold' is merely a form,
variety, and rate of vibration. So 'heat' and 'cold' are
simply the 'two poles' of that which we call

'heat'—and the phenomena attendant thereupon are manifestations of the principle of polarity. The same principle manifests in the case of 'light and darkness', which are the same thing, the difference consisting of varying degrees between the two poles of the phenomena. Where does 'darkness' leave off, and 'light' begin? What is the difference between 'large and small'? Between 'hard and soft'? Between 'black and white'? Between 'sharp and dull'? Between 'noise and quiet'? Between 'high and low'? Between 'positive and negative'? The principle of polarity explains these paradoxes, and no other principle can supersede it. The same principle operates on the mental plane. Let us take a radical and extreme example—that of 'love and hate', two mental states apparently totally different. And yet there are degrees of hate and degrees of love, and a middle point in which we use the terms 'like or dislike', which shade into each other so gradually that sometimes we are at a loss to know whether we 'like' or 'dislike' or 'neither'. And all are simply degrees of the same thing, as you will see if you will but think a moment. And, more than this (and considered of more importance by the Hermetists), it is possible to change the vibrations of hate to the vibrations of love, in one's own mind, and in the minds of others. Many of you, who read these lines, have had personal experiences of the involuntary rapid transition from love to hate, and the reverse, in your own case and that of others. And you will therefore realize the possibility of this being accomplished by the use of the will, by means of the Hermetic formulas. 'Good and evil' are but the poles of the same thing, and the Hermetist understands the art of transmuting evil into good, by means of an application of the principle of polarity. In short, the 'art of polarization' becomes a phase of 'mental alchemy' known and practiced by the ancient and modern Hermetic masters. An understanding of the principle will enable one to change his own polarity, as well as that of others, if he will devote the time and study necessary to master the art.

5. THE PRINCIPLE OF RHYTHM

'Everything flows, out and in; everything has its tides; all things rise and fall; the pendulum-swing manifests in everything; the measure of the swing to the right is the measure of the swing to the left; rhythm compensates.'—The Kybalion.

This principle embodies the truth that in everything there is manifested a measured motion, to and fro; a flow and inflow; a swing backward and forward; a pendulum-like movement; a tide-like ebb and flow; a high-tide and low-tide; between the two poles which exist in accordance with the principle of polarity described a moment ago. There is always an action and a reaction; an advance and a retreat; a rising and a sinking. This is in the affairs of the universe, suns, worlds, men, animals, mind, energy, and matter. This law is manifest in the creation and destruction of worlds; in the rise and fall of nations; in the life of all things; and finally in the mental states of man (and it is with this latter that the Hermetists find the understanding of the principle most important). The Hermetists have grasped this principle, finding its universal application, and have also discovered certain means to overcome its effects in themselves by the use of the appropriate formulas and methods. They apply the mental law of neutralization. They cannot annul the principle, or cause it to cease its operation, but they have learned how to escape its effects upon themselves to a certain degree depending upon the mastery of the principle. They have learned how to *use* it, instead of being *used by* it. In this and similar methods, consist the art of the Hermetists. The master of Hermetics polarizes himself at the point at which he desires to rest, and then neutralizes the rhythmic swing of the pendulum which would tend to carry him to the other pole. All individuals who have attained any degree of self-mastery do this to a certain degree, more or less unconsciously, but the master does this consciously, and by the use of his will, and attains a degree of poise and mental firmness almost impossible of belief on the part of the masses who are swung backward and forward like a pendulum. This principle and that of polarity have been closely studied by the Hermetists, and the methods of counteracting, neutralizing, and *using* them form an important part of the Hermetic mental alchemy.

6. THE PRINCIPLE OF CAUSE AND EFFECT

'Every cause has its effect; every effect has its cause; everything happens according to law; chance is but a name for law not recognized; there are many planes of causation, but nothing escapes the law.'—The Kybalion.

This principle embodies the fact that there is a cause for every effect; an effect from every cause. It explains that: 'Everything happens according to law'; that nothing ever 'merely happens'; that there is no such thing as chance; that while there are various planes of cause and effect, the higher dominating the lower planes, still nothing ever entirely escapes the law. The Hermetists understand the art and methods of rising above the ordinary plane of cause and effect, to a certain degree, and by mentally rising to a higher plane they become causers instead of effects. The masses of people are carried along, obedient to environment; the wills and desires of others stronger than themselves; heredity; suggestion; and other outward causes moving them about like pawns on the chessboard of life. But the masters, rising to the plane above, dominate their moods, characters, qualities, and powers, as well as the environment surrounding them, and become movers instead of pawns. They help to *play the game of life*, instead of being played and moved about by other wills and environment. They *use* the principle instead of being its tools. The masters obey the causation of the higher planes, but they help to *rule* on their own plane. In this statement there is condensed a wealth of Hermetic knowledge—let him read who can.

7. THE PRINCIPLE OF GENDER

'*Gender is in everything; everything has its masculine and feminine principles; gender manifests on all planes.*'—*The Kybalion.*

This principle embodies the truth that there is *gender* manifested in everything—the masculine and feminine principles ever at work. This is true not only of the physical plane, but of the mental and even the spiritual planes. On the physical plane, the principle manifests as *sex*, on the higher planes it takes higher forms, but the principle is ever the same. No creation, physical, mental, or spiritual, is possible without this principle. An understanding of its laws will throw light on many a subject that has perplexed the minds of men. The principle of gender works ever in the direction of generation, regeneration, and creation. Everything, and every person, contains the two elements or principles, or this great principle, within it, him or her. Every male thing has the female element also; every female contains also the male principle. If you would understand the philosophy of mental and spiritual creation, generation, and re-generation, you must understand and study this Hermetic principle. It contains the solution of many mysteries of life. We caution you that this principle has no reference to the many base, pernicious, and degrading lustful theories, teachings, and practices, which are taught under fanciful titles, and which are a prostitution of the great natural principle of gender. Such base revivals of the ancient infamous forms of phallicism tend to ruin mind, body, and soul, and the Hermetic philosophy has ever sounded the warning note against these degraded teachings which tend toward lust, licentiousness, and perversion of nature's principles. If you seek such teachings, you must go elsewhere for them—Hermeticism contains nothing for you along these lines. To the pure, all things are pure; to the base, all things are base.

2

ECCLESIASTES

Introduction

Ecclesiastes has a title that makes it sound like every schoolboy's nightmare: dry, preachy, and remote—'ecclesiastical'.

In fact, this is one of the more intriguing of the books of the Bible and offers a perspective that can be shared by believers, non-believers, and heretics alike.

Ecclesiastes falls squarely within the 'wisdom literature' of the Bible—the class of Hebrew writings that deal with general ethical and religious questions, as distinct from prophetic or liturgical literature. The wisdom literature provides detached and sage observations on the deep problems of life. It is, admittedly, not always easy to make the Bible relevant and attractive today. Ecclesiastes, however, *is* able to reach out to the modern reader. In some ways, it is shocking in its brutal honesty.

The author is King Solomon and the work consists of his musings on life and the lessons he has been able to draw from it. The King wants to answer the question: 'What should man do during his time "under the sun" (on the earth)?' He looks back on the ways he has attempted to find happiness. First, he tried to increase his learning and wisdom—but this didn't work since to increase wisdom is only to increase sorrow, and thus a kind of 'chasing after wind'. Next, he tried pleasure, but this too was foolishness and vanity, and accomplished nothing. Finally, he attempted to find happiness by application of his great wealth: building houses, gardens, and parks, planting vineyards, and buying servants and musicians. It made no difference that the King's expenditure was directed towards constructive goals. It was all 'chasing after the wind' with no profit to him 'under the sun'.

It is at this point that we expect the turnaround: we expect that Solomon will find reassurance in his faith and in God.

But that's not what happens.

Instead, the King goes to a darker place. True, he observes, a wise man can see, whereas a fool walks in darkness. But what does that matter? Both meet the same end—both will die. And after death, to whom do we leave the products of all our hard work? To 'the man who comes after'. But who knows whether our descendants will be wise men or fools? All is vanity, then, and while alive on earth, man cannot know what is good for him to do.

The still more brutal truth follows next. For the King admits that just as we know nothing of God's reasons for creating life on earth, we know nothing of what will come after. For him who is living there is hope, but for the dead there is none: 'For the living know that they will die, but the dead don't know anything, neither do they have any more a reward; for the memory of them is forgotten.' The love, hatred, and envy of the dead have perished—they have no part to play in the affairs of the living. A living dog, concludes the King, is better than a dead lion.

What is left for man is to live—to live bravely and boldly. Eat with joy, says the King, and drink with a merry heart. Live out your days of vanity with the wife whom you love with all your heart. And whenever your hands find work to do, do it with all your might.

Ecclesiastes is the great rebel text of the bible. There is no hiding from the reality of life's great mystery here. The meaning of existence is incomprehensible to man and is experienced as pure vanity or, in the evocative words of King Solomon in Ecclesiastes, 'chasing after the wind'.

For the modern man, Ecclesiastes communicates the truth rarely acknowledged in any era—but still more rarely acknowledged in our own—that enduring happiness is something that lies forever out of reach. In place of happiness, we find something more compelling: the glimpse of a man determined to work and live with all his might in full knowledge that nothing can come from it—at least, nothing in the way of worldly happiness. What Solomon achieves instead is dignity, power, and a kind of dark charisma. The trade-off is not, perhaps, so bad after all.

ECCLESIASTES

1. The words of the Preacher, the son of David, king in Jerusalem: 'Vanity of vanities,' says the Preacher; 'Vanity of vanities, all is vanity.' What does man gain from all his labour in which he labours under the sun? One generation goes, and another generation comes; but the earth remains forever. The sun also rises, and the sun goes down, and hurries to its place where it rises. The wind goes toward the south, and turns around to the north. It turns around continually as it goes, and the wind returns again to its courses. All the rivers run into the sea, yet the sea is not full. To the place where the rivers flow, there they flow again. All things are full of weariness beyond uttering. The eye is not satisfied with seeing, nor the ear filled with hearing. That which has been is that which shall be; and that which has been done is that which shall be done: and there is no new thing under the sun. Is there a thing of which it may be said, 'Behold, this is new?' It has been long ago, in

the ages which were before us. There is no memory of the former; neither shall there be any memory of the latter that are to come, among those that shall come after.

I, the Preacher, was king over Israel in Jerusalem. I applied my heart to seek and to search out by wisdom concerning all that is done under the sky. It is a heavy burden that God has given to the sons of men to be afflicted with. I have seen all the works that are done under the sun; and behold, all is vanity and a chasing after wind. That which is crooked can't be made straight; and that which is lacking can't be counted. I said to myself, 'Behold, I have obtained for myself great wisdom above all who were before me in Jerusalem. Yes, my heart has had great experience of wisdom and knowledge.' I applied my heart to know wisdom, and to know madness and folly. I perceived that this also was a chasing after wind. For in much wisdom is much grief; and he who increases knowledge increases sorrow.

2. I said in my heart, 'Come now, I will test you with mirth: therefore enjoy pleasure'; and behold, this also was vanity. I said of laughter, 'It is foolishness'; and of mirth, 'What does it accomplish?'

I searched in my heart how to cheer my flesh with wine, my heart yet guiding me with wisdom, and how to lay hold of folly, until I might see what it was good for the sons of men that they should do under heaven all the days of their lives. I made myself great works. I built myself houses. I planted myself vineyards. I made myself gardens and parks, and I planted trees in them of all kinds of fruit. I made myself pools of water, to water from it the forest where trees were reared. I bought male servants and female servants, and had servants born in my house. I also had great possessions of herds and flocks, above all who were before me in Jerusalem; I also gathered silver and gold for myself, and the treasure of kings and of the provinces. I got myself male and female singers, and the delights of the sons of men—musical instruments, and that of all sorts. So I was great, and increased more than all who were before me in Jerusalem. My wisdom also remained with me. Whatever my eyes desired, I didn't keep from them. I didn't withhold my heart from any joy, for my heart rejoiced because of all my labour, and this was my portion from all my labour. Then I looked at all the works that my hands had worked, and at the labour that I had laboured to do; and behold, all was vanity and a chasing after wind, and there was no profit under the sun.

I turned myself to consider wisdom, madness, and folly: for what can the king's successor do? Just that which has been done long ago. Then I saw that wisdom excels folly, as far as light excels darkness. The wise man's eyes are in his head, and the fool walks in darkness—and yet I perceived that one event happens to them all. Then said I in my heart, 'As it happens to the fool, so will it happen even to me; and why was I then more wise?' Then said I in my heart that this also is vanity. For of the wise man, even as of the fool, there is no memory for ever, seeing that in the days to come all will have been long forgotten. Indeed, the wise man must die just like the fool!

So I hated life, because the work that is worked under the sun was grievous to me; for all is vanity and a chasing after wind. I hated all my labour in which I laboured under the sun, seeing that I must leave it to the man who comes after me. Who knows whether he will be a wise man or a fool? Yet he will have rule over all of my labour in which I have laboured, and in which I have shown myself wise under the sun. This also is vanity.

Therefore I began to cause my heart to despair concerning all the labour in which I had laboured under the sun. For there is a man whose labour is with wisdom, with knowledge, and with skillfulness; yet he shall leave it for his portion to a man who has not laboured for it. This also is vanity and a great evil. For what has a man of all his labour, and of the striving of his heart, in which he labours under the sun? For all his days are sorrows, and his travail is grief; yes, even in the night his heart takes no rest. This also is vanity. There is nothing better for a man than that he should eat and drink, and make his soul enjoy good in his labour. This also I saw, that it is from the hand of God. For who can eat, or who can have enjoyment, more than I? For to the man who pleases him, God gives wisdom, knowledge, and joy; but to the sinner he gives travail, to gather and to heap up, that he may give to him who pleases God. This also is vanity and a chasing after wind.

3. For everything there is a season, and a time for every purpose under heaven:

a time to be born,
and a time to die;
a time to plant,
and a time to pluck up that which is planted;
a time to kill,
and a time to heal;
a time to break down,
and a time to build up;
a time to weep,
and a time to laugh;
a time to mourn,
and a time to dance;
a time to cast away stones,
and a time to gather stones together;
a time to embrace,
and a time to refrain from embracing;
a time to seek,
and a time to lose;
a time to keep,
and a time to cast away;
a time to tear,
and a time to sew;
a time to keep silence,
and a time to speak;
a time to love,
and a time to hate;

a time for war,
and a time for peace.

...

9. For all this I laid to my heart, even to explore all this: that the righteous, and the wise, and their works, are in the hand of God; whether it is love or hatred, man doesn't know it; all is before them. All things come alike to all. There is one event to the righteous and to the wicked; to the good, to the clean, to the unclean, to him who sacrifices, and to him who doesn't sacrifice. As is the good, so is the sinner; he who takes an oath, as he who fears an oath. This is an evil in all that is done under the sun, that there is one event to all: yes also, the heart of the sons of men is full of evil, and madness is in their heart while they live, and after that they go to the dead. For to him who is joined with all the living there is hope; for a living dog is better than a dead lion. For the living know that they will die, but the dead don't know anything, neither do they have any more a reward; for the memory of them is forgotten. Also their love, their hatred, and their envy has perished long ago; neither have they any more a portion forever in anything that is done under the sun.

Go your way—eat your bread with joy, and drink your wine with a merry heart; for God has already accepted your works. Let your garments be always white, and don't let your head lack oil. Live joyfully with the wife whom you love all the days of your life of vanity, which he has given you under the sun, all your days of vanity: for that is your portion in life, and in your labour in which you labour under the sun. Whatever your hand finds to do, do it with your might; for there is no work, nor device, nor knowledge, nor wisdom, in Sheol, where you are going.

I returned, and saw under the sun, that the race is not to the swift, nor the battle to the strong, neither yet bread to the wise, nor yet riches to men of understanding, nor yet favour to men of skill; but time and chance happen to them all.

LAO-TZU, TAO TE CHING

INTRODUCTION

Taoism as a spiritual path is focussed on identifying and drawing upon the primordial force that flows through all things, and on bringing our lives into harmony with it.

Taoism (or Daoism as it is also known) refers to that primordial force as the 'Tao' (or 'Dao')—literally, the 'Way'. It is fundamental that the Tao is nameless and defies easy conceptualization. But that doesn't mean that nothing can be said about it.

In one view, the Tao refers to the essential force or energy which expands from an original unity into the multiplicity of things we find in the universe. The One gives way to the two, yin (receptive, dark, female) and yang (active, light, male), which interact to give way to the three principal aspects of the universe: heaven, earth, and humankind. From these three comes the endless diversity of existence.

In another view, the Tao is the mysterious 'nothing' or non-being which is the transcendent ground of all things. Everything originates from nothing and returns to nothing. The Tao is like the eye of a tornado: an empty originating point surrounded by the activity of existence.

More recently, the Tao has been considered as the self-generating order found within, and governing, the natural world.

The key figure in Taoism is an ancient Chinese sage by the name of Lao-tzu (or Laozi)—literally, 'Old Master'. Lao-tzu is believed to have lived in the 6th century BC and was a contemporary of Confucius. It is said that when he retired from the court, where he had been working as an archivist, he set off on a journey west, but was stopped at the Hangu Pass by the gatekeeper there who asked him to compose a text outlining his philosophy. What he came up with was the *Tao Te Ching* (or *Daode jing*), the philosophy of way (*tao*) and power (*te*). The legend has it that Lao-tzu travelled onwards to India, where he appeared as the Buddha, and to the far west where he appeared as Mani, founder of a dualistic Christian sect. Lao-tzu was said to be a manifestation of the Tao itself.

Taoism went on to become an organized religion of several lineages, some focussing on intercession with spiritual forces and others emphasizing internal meditative and energy practices.

Nevertheless, it remains the texts themselves that provide the raw materials for heightening of spiritual awareness.

The *Tao Te Ching* is the wellspring of the tradition and it returns again and again to several essential themes. The Tao, it says, is the original spontaneous and self-generating source of power in a universe of constant transformation. The way to release the power of the Tao is to allow the intrinsic virtue or nature of a thing to flourish. The more we seek to impose our own will on things, and distort or inhibit this natural flourishing, the further removed we become from the Tao, and the further our societies descend into tyranny and disorder. The enlightened ruler or sage, on the other hand, cultivates spontaneity within himself and his followers which radiates outwards through society as a whole.

The *Tao Te Ching* has a unique value for the modern man. Our age is characterised by make-work, busy-ness, and reflex interventionism. We rarely pause to question the efficacy of all this: *more* is routinely and unquestioningly perceived to be *better*. The *Tao Te Ching* offers another approach premised upon the flourishing of intrinsic potential. It is an approach that is fresh, minimalistic, and uncluttered. Act judiciously and with restraint, it suggests. Conserve energy. And know that there is an immense power that is yours to access by bringing yourself into harmony with the true nature of being.

PART 1

CHAPTER 1

The Tao that can be trodden is not the enduring and unchanging Tao. The name that can be named is not the enduring and unchanging name.

Conceived of as having no name, it is the originator of heaven and earth; conceived of as having a name, it is the mother of all things.

Always without desire we must be found,
If its deep mystery we would sound;
But if desire always within us be,
Its outer fringe is all that we shall see.

Under these two aspects, it is really the same; but as development takes place, it receives the different names. Together we call them the mystery. Where the mystery is the deepest is the gate of all that is subtle and wonderful.

CHAPTER 2

All in the world know the beauty of the beautiful, and in doing this they have the idea of what ugliness is; they all know the skill of the skilful, and in doing this they have the idea of what the want of skill is.

So it is that existence and non-existence give birth the one to the idea of the other; that difficulty and ease produce the one the idea of the other; that length and shortness fashion out of the one the figure of the other; that the ideas of height and lowness arise from the contrast of the one with the other; that the musical notes and tones become harmonious through the relation of one with another; and that being before and behind give the idea of one following another.

Therefore the sage manages affairs without doing anything, and conveys his instructions without the use of speech.

All things spring up, and there is not one which declines to show itself; they grow, and there is no claim made for their ownership; they go through their processes, and there is no expectation of a reward for the results. The work is accomplished, and there is no resting in it as an achievement.

The work is done, but how no one can see;
'Tis this that makes the power not cease to be.

CHAPTER 3

Not to value and employ men of superior ability is the way to keep the people from rivalry among themselves; not to prize articles which are difficult to procure is the way to keep them from becoming thieves; not to show them what is likely to excite their desires is the way to keep their minds from disorder.

Therefore the sage, in the exercise of his government, empties their minds, fills their bellies, weakens their wills, and strengthens their bones.

He constantly tries to keep them without knowledge and without desire, and where there are those who have knowledge, to keep them from presuming to act on it. When there is this abstinence from action, good order is universal.

CHAPTER 4

The Tao is like the emptiness of a vessel; and in our employment of it we must be on our guard against all fulness. How deep and unfathomable it is, as if it were the honoured ancestor of all things!

We should blunt our sharp points, and unravel the complications of things; we should attemper our brightness, and bring ourselves into agreement with the obscurity of others. How pure and still the Tao is, as if it would ever so continue!

I do not know whose son it is. It might appear to have been before God.

CHAPTER 5

Heaven and earth do not act from the impulse of any wish to be benevolent; they deal with all things as the dogs of grass[1] are dealt with. The sages do not act from any wish to be benevolent; they deal with the people as the dogs of grass are dealt with.

May not the space between heaven and earth be compared to a bellows?

'Tis emptied, yet it loses not its power;
'Tis moved again, and sends forth air the more.
Much speech to swift exhaustion lead we see;
Your inner being guard, and keep it free.

CHAPTER 6

The valley spirit dies not, aye the same;
The female mystery thus do we name.
Its gate, from which at first they issued forth,
Is called the root from which grew heaven and earth.
Long and unbroken does its power remain,
Used gently, and without the touch of pain.

1. Straw tied up in the shape of dogs used in praying for rain; when the sacrifice was over the straw dogs were thrown aside and left uncared for.

41

CHAPTER 7

Heaven is long-enduring and earth continues long. The reason why heaven and earth are able to endure and continue thus long is because they do not live of, or for, themselves. This is how they are able to continue and endure.

Therefore the sage puts his own person last, and yet it is found in the foremost place; he treats his person as if it were foreign to him, and yet that person is preserved. Is it not because he has no personal and private ends, that therefore such ends are realised?

CHAPTER 8

The highest excellence is like that of water. The excellence of water appears in its benefiting all things, and in its occupying, without striving to the contrary, the low place which all men dislike. Hence its way is near to that of the Tao.

The excellence of a residence is in the suitability of the place; that of the mind is in abysmal stillness; that of associations is in their being with the virtuous; that of government is in its securing good order; that of the conduct of affairs is in its ability; and that of the initiation of any movement is in its timeliness.

And when one with the highest excellence does

not wrangle about his low position, no one finds fault with him.

CHAPTER 9

It is better to leave a vessel unfilled, than to attempt to carry it when it is full. If you keep feeling a point that has been sharpened, the point cannot long preserve its sharpness.

When gold and jade fill the hall, their possessor cannot keep them safe. When wealth and honours lead to arrogancy, this brings its evil on itself. When the work is done, and one's name is becoming distinguished, to withdraw into obscurity is the way of Heaven.

CHAPTER 10

When the intelligent and animal souls are held together in one embrace, they can be kept from separating. When one gives undivided attention to the vital breath, and brings it to the utmost degree of pliancy, he can become as a tender babe. When he has cleansed away the most mysterious sights of his imagination, he can become without a flaw.

In loving the people and ruling the state, cannot he proceed without any purpose of action? In the opening and shutting of his gates of heaven, cannot he do so as a female bird? While his intelligence reaches in every direction, cannot he appear to be without knowledge?

The Tao produces all things and nourishes them; it produces them and does not claim them as its own; it does all, and yet does not boast of it; it presides over all, and yet does not control them. This is what is called 'the mysterious quality' of the Tao.

CHAPTER 11

The thirty spokes unite in the one nave; but it is on the empty space for the axle that the use of the wheel depends. Clay is fashioned into vessels; but it is on their empty hollowness that their use depends. The door and windows are cut out from the walls to form an apartment; but it is on the empty space within that its use depends. Therefore, what has a positive existence serves for profitable adaptation, and what has not that for actual usefulness.

CHAPTER 16

The state of vacancy should be brought to the utmost degree, and that of stillness guarded with unwearying vigour. All things alike go through their processes of activity, and then we see them return to their original state. When things in the vegetable world have displayed their luxuriant growth, we see each of them return to its root. This returning to their root is what we call the state of stillness; and that stillness may be called a reporting that they have fulfilled their appointed end.

The report of that fulfilment is the regular, unchanging rule. To know that unchanging rule is to be intelligent; not to know it leads to wild movements and evil issues. The knowledge of that unchanging rule produces a grand capacity and forbearance, and that capacity and forbearance lead to a community of feeling with all things. From this community of feeling comes a kingliness of character; and he who is king-like goes on to be heaven-like. In that likeness to heaven he possesses the Tao. Possessed of the Tao, he endures long; and to the end of his bodily life, is exempt from all danger of decay.

CHAPTER 18

When the Great Tao (Way or Method) ceased to be observed, benevolence and righteousness came into vogue. Then appeared wisdom and shrewdness, and there ensued great hypocrisy.

When harmony no longer prevailed throughout the six kinships, filial sons found their manifestation; when the states and clans fell into disorder, loyal ministers appeared.

CHAPTER 26

Gravity is the root of lightness; stillness, the ruler of movement.

Therefore a wise prince, marching the whole day, does not go far from his baggage waggons. Although he may have brilliant prospects to look at, he quietly remains in his proper place, indifferent to them. How should the lord of a myriad chariots carry himself lightly before the kingdom? If he do act lightly, he has lost his root of gravity; if he proceed to active movement, he will lose his throne.

CHAPTER 29

If anyone should wish to get the kingdom for himself, and to effect this by what he does, I see that he will not succeed. The kingdom is a spirit-like thing, and cannot be got by active doing. He who would so win it destroys it; he who would hold it in his grasp loses it.

> *The course and nature of things is such that*
> *What was in front is now behind;*
> *What warmed anon we freezing find.*
> *Strength is of weakness oft the spoil;*
> *The store in ruins mocks our toil.*

Hence the sage puts away excessive effort, extravagance, and easy indulgence.

CHAPTER 33

He who knows other men is discerning; he who knows himself is intelligent. He who overcomes others is strong; he who overcomes himself is mighty. He who is satisfied with his lot is rich; he who goes on acting with energy has a firm will.

He who does not fail in the requirements of his position, continues long; he who dies and yet does not perish, has longevity.

Part 2

CHAPTER 43

The softest thing in the world dashes against and overcomes the hardest; that which has no substantial existence enters where there is no crevice. I know hereby what advantage belongs to doing nothing with a purpose.

There are few in the world who attain to the teaching without words, and the advantage arising from non-action.

CHAPTER 57

A state may be ruled by measures of correction; weapons of war may be used with crafty dexterity; but the kingdom is made one's own only by freedom from action and purpose.

How do I know that it is so? By these facts: in the kingdom the multiplication of prohibitive enactments increases the poverty of the people; the more implements to add to their profit that the people have, the greater disorder is there in the state and clan; the more acts of crafty dexterity that men possess, the more do strange contrivances appear; the more display there is of legislation, the more thieves and robbers there are.

Therefore a sage has said, 'I will do nothing of purpose, and the people will be transformed of themselves; I will be fond of keeping still, and the people will of themselves become correct. I will take no trouble about it, and the people will of themselves become rich; I will manifest no ambition, and the people will of themselves attain to the primitive simplicity.'

CHAPTER 63

It is the way of the Tao to act without thinking of acting; to conduct affairs without feeling the trouble of them; to taste without discerning any flavour; to consider what is small as great, and a few as many; and to recompense injury with kindness.

The master of it anticipates things that are difficult while they are easy, and does things that would become great while they are small. All difficult things in the world are sure to arise from a previous state in which they were easy, and all great things from one in which they were small. Therefore the sage, while he never does what is great, is able on that account to accomplish the greatest things.

He who lightly promises is sure to keep but little faith; he who is continually thinking things easy is sure to find them difficult. Therefore the sage sees difficulty even in what seems easy, and so never has any difficulties.

CHAPTER 64

That which is at rest is easily kept hold of; before a thing has given indications of its presence, it is easy to take measures against it; that which is brittle is easily broken; that which is very small is easily dispersed. Action should be taken before a thing has made its appearance; order should be secured before disorder has begun.

The tree which fills the arms grew from the tiniest sprout; the tower of nine storeys rose from a small heap of earth; the journey of a thousand li commenced with a single step.

He who acts with an ulterior purpose does harm; he who takes hold of a thing in the same way loses his hold. The sage does not act so, and therefore does no harm; he does not lay hold so, and therefore does not lose his hold. But people in their conduct of affairs are constantly ruining them when they are on the eve of success. If they were careful at the end, as they should be at the beginning, they would not so ruin them.

Therefore the sage desires what other men do not desire, and does not prize things difficult to get; he learns what other men do not learn, and turns back to what the multitude of men have passed by. Thus he helps the natural development of all things, and does not dare to act with an ulterior purpose of his own.

CHAPTER 65

The ancients who showed their skill in practising the Tao did so, not to enlighten the people, but rather to make them simple and ignorant.

The difficulty in governing the people arises from their having much knowledge. He who tries to govern a state by his wisdom is a scourge to it; while he who does not try to do so is a blessing.

He who knows these two things finds in them also his model and rule. Ability to know this model and rule constitutes what we call the mysterious excellence of a governor. Deep and far-reaching is such mysterious excellence, showing indeed its possessor as opposite to others, but leading them to a great conformity to him.

CHAPTER 66

That whereby the rivers and seas are able to receive the homage and tribute of all the valley streams, is their skill in being lower than they—it is thus that they are the kings of them all. So it is that the sage ruler, wishing to be above men, puts himself by his words below them, and, wishing to be before them, places his person behind them.

In this way though he has his place above them, men do not feel his weight, nor though he has his place before them, do they feel it an injury to them.

Therefore all in the world delight to exalt him and do not weary of him. Because he does not strive, no one finds it possible to strive with him.

CHAPTER 77

May not the Way (or Tao) of Heaven be compared to the method of bending a bow? The part of the bow which was high is brought low, and what was low is raised up. So Heaven diminishes where there is superabundance, and supplements where there is deficiency.

It is the Way of Heaven to diminish

superabundance, and to supplement deficiency. It is not so with the way of man. He takes away from those who have not enough to add to his own superabundance.

Who can take his own superabundance and therewith serve all under heaven? Only he who is in possession of the Tao!

Therefore the ruling sage acts without claiming the results as his; he achieves his merit and does not rest arrogantly in it—he does not wish to display his superiority.

CHAPTER 78

There is nothing in the world more soft and weak than water, and yet for attacking things that are firm and strong there is nothing that can take precedence of it—for there is nothing so effectual for which it can be changed.

Everyone in the world knows that the soft overcomes the hard, and the weak the strong, but no one is able to carry it out in practice.

CHAPTER 81

Sincere words are not fine; fine words are not sincere. Those who are skilled in the Tao do not dispute about it; the disputatious are not skilled in it. Those who know the Tao are not extensively learned; the extensively learned do not know it.

The sage does not accumulate for himself. The more that he expends for others, the more does he possess of his own; the more that he gives to others, the more does he have himself.

With all the sharpness of the Way of Heaven, it injures not; with all the doing in the way of the sage he does not strive.

BUDDHA, THE DHAMMAPADA

INTRODUCTION

Once there was a woman by the name of Krisha Gautami whose only son had died. In her immense grief, she carried her dead child to all her neighbours, asking them for medicine. 'She has lost her senses,' said the people. 'The boy is dead.' Eventually, she met a man who responded to her request. 'I cannot give you medicine for your child, but I know a physician who can.' The girl said: 'Tell me sir: Who is it?' The man replied: 'Go to Sakyamuni, the Buddha.'

So Krisha Gautami went to the Buddha and pleaded: 'Lord and Master, give me the medicine that will cure my boy.' The Buddha answered: 'I want a handful of mustard seed.' When the woman in her joy promised to get hold of it, the Buddha added: 'The mustard seed must be taken from a house where no one has died.' So poor Krisha Gautami went from house to house, and the people pitied her, saying: 'Here is mustard seed—take it.' But when she asked if anyone had died there, the people could only answer: 'Alas the living are few, but the dead are many. Do not remind us of our deepest grief.' There was not one house in which someone's beloved had not died.

On realizing this, Krisha Gautami buried her dead child in the forest and sought refuge in the Buddha and in his teachings.

The tale of Krisha Gautami reflects the core of the Buddha's message: that suffering exists; that suffering arises from attachment to desires; that suffering ceases when attachment to desire ceases; and that freedom from suffering is possible by practising the Buddhist teachings.

For the most striking and accessible account of those teachings, we can turn to the *Dhammapada*.

Dhammapada means 'the path of dharma'—the path of truth, of righteousness, and of doctrine. It is a collection of the sayings of the Buddha spoken on various occasions. In its bold lucidity, it makes the Buddhist way of life accessible to all.

What does it have to say to the modern man?

The first and most powerful point is that our thoughts determine our destiny. 'All that we are,' says the Buddha, 'is a result of what we have thought: it is founded on our thoughts, it is made up of our thoughts.' In a sense this gives rise to the most basic

principle of *karma* or destiny: if you speak or act with
a pure thought, happiness will follow, whereas if you
speak or act with an evil thought, pain will follow,
as a matter of cause and effect. However, to steady
trembling and unsteady thoughts is as difficult as to
steady an arrow in a bow. The most dangerous
thoughts are those that allow us to paint ourselves
as eternal victims: 'He abused me, he beat me, he
defeated me, he robbed me.' In those who harbour
such thoughts, warns the Buddha, hatred will never
cease.

This leads directly to the second point: the
importance of taking full responsibility for yourself.
'Self is the lord of self,' teaches the Buddha. 'Who else
could be the lord?' Much is packed into this: you are
lord of yourself—no-one and nothing else can usurp
that position. Direct yourself properly first, teaches
the Buddha. Only then can you begin to help others.
There is no room for moralistic meddling or for
premature philanthropy here: 'Let no one forget his
own duty for the sake of another's.'

The third aspect of the Buddha's teaching is the
importance of facing up to the basic realities of
existence and to what life has in store. 'All created
things perish,' says the Buddha, all life ends in 'griefs
and pains', and the forms we meet with are all
transitory and at root unreal. If you can look at your
own predicament squarely in the face—with no
flinching and no backtracking—then you have

achieved something that will give you a depth and a gravitas that is as powerful as it is rare.

Buddhism is a philosophy and a faith marked indelibly by its origin in the elite warrior-caste: the Buddha himself, Siddhartha Gautama, was born into the aristocracy and was said to have been originally destined to be a king. Buddhism, accordingly, doesn't demand your submission; it recalls you to the intrinsic nobility of your basic nature. What could be more valuable, or more necessary, for the modern man?

———

CHAPTER I. THE TWIN-VERSES

1. All that we are is the result of what we have thought: it is founded on our thoughts, it is made up of our thoughts. If a man speaks or acts with an evil thought, pain follows him, as the wheel follows the foot of the ox that draws the carriage.

2. All that we are is the result of what we have thought: it is founded on our thoughts, it is made up of our thoughts. If a man speaks or acts with a pure thought, happiness follows him, like a shadow that never leaves him.

3. 'He abused me, he beat me, he defeated me, he robbed me'—in those who harbour such thoughts hatred will never cease.

4. 'He abused me, he beat me, he defeated me, he

robbed me'—in those who do not harbour such thoughts hatred will cease.

5. For hatred does not cease by hatred at any time: hatred ceases by love, this is an old rule.

6. The world does not know that we must all come to an end here; but those who know it, their quarrels cease at once.

7. He who lives looking for pleasures only, his senses uncontrolled, immoderate in his food, idle, and weak, Mara (the tempter) will certainly overthrow him, as the wind throws down a weak tree.

8. He who lives without looking for pleasures, his senses well controlled, moderate in his food, faithful and strong, him Mara will certainly not overthrow, any more than the wind throws down a rocky mountain.

9. He who wishes to put on the yellow dress without having cleansed himself from sin, who disregards temperance and truth, is unworthy of the yellow dress.

10. But he who has cleansed himself from sin, is well grounded in all virtues, and regards also temperance and truth, he is indeed worthy of the yellow dress.

11. They who imagine truth in untruth, and see untruth in truth, never arrive at truth, but follow vain desires.

12. They who know truth in truth, and untruth in untruth, arrive at truth, and follow true desires.

13. As rain breaks through an ill-thatched house, passion will break through an unreflecting mind.

14. As rain does not break through a well-thatched house, passion will not break through a well-reflecting mind.

15. The evil-doer mourns in this world, and he mourns in the next; he mourns in both. He mourns and suffers when he sees the evil of his own work.

16. The virtuous man delights in this world, and he delights in the next; he delights in both. He delights and rejoices, when he sees the purity of his own work.

17. The evil-doer suffers in this world, and he suffers in the next; he suffers in both. He suffers when he thinks of the evil he has done; he suffers more when going on the evil path.

18. The virtuous man is happy in this world, and he is happy in the next; he is happy in both. He is happy when he thinks of the good he has done; he is still more happy when going on the good path.

19. The thoughtless man, even if he can recite a large portion of the law, but is not a doer of it, has no share in the priesthood, but is like a cowherd counting the cows of others.

20. The follower of the law, even if he can recite only a small portion of the law, but, having forsaken passion and hatred and foolishness, possesses true knowledge and serenity of mind, he, caring for nothing in this world or that to come, has indeed a share in the priesthood.

CHAPTER II. ON EARNESTNESS

21. Earnestness is the path of immortality (Nirvana), thoughtlessness the path of death. Those who are in earnest do not die, those who are thoughtless are as if dead already.

22. Those who are advanced in earnestness, having understood this clearly, delight in earnestness, and rejoice in the knowledge of the Ariyas (the elect).

23. These wise people, meditative, steady, always possessed of strong powers, attain to Nirvana, the highest happiness.

24. If an earnest person has roused himself, if he is not forgetful, if his deeds are pure, if he acts with consideration, if he restrains himself, and lives according to law, then his glory will increase.

25. By rousing himself, by earnestness, by restraint and control, the wise man may make for himself an island which no flood can overwhelm.

26. Fools follow after vanity, men of evil wisdom. The wise man keeps earnestness as his best jewel.

27. Follow not after vanity, nor after the enjoyment of love and lust! He who is earnest and meditative, obtains ample joy.

28. When the learned man drives away vanity by earnestness, he, the wise, climbing the terraced heights of wisdom, looks down upon the fools, serene he looks upon the toiling crowd, as one that stands on a mountain looks down upon them that stand upon the plain.

29. Earnest among the thoughtless, awake among the sleepers, the wise man advances like a racer, leaving behind the hack.

30. By earnestness did Maghavan (Indra) rise to the lordship of the gods. People praise earnestness; thoughtlessness is always blamed.

31. A Bhikshu (mendicant) who delights in earnestness, who looks with fear on thoughtlessness, moves about like fire, burning all his fetters, small or large.

32. A Bhikshu (mendicant) who delights in reflection, who looks with fear on thoughtlessness, cannot fall away from his perfect state—he is close upon Nirvana.

Chapter III. Thought

33. As a fletcher makes straight his arrow, a wise man makes straight his trembling and unsteady thought, which is difficult to guard, difficult to hold back.

34. As a fish taken from his watery home and thrown on dry ground, our thought trembles all over in order to escape the dominion of Mara (the tempter).

35. It is good to tame the mind, which is difficult to hold in and flighty, rushing wherever it listeth; a tamed mind brings happiness.

36. Let the wise man guard his thoughts, for they are difficult to perceive, very artful, and they rush

wherever they list: thoughts well guarded bring happiness.

37. Those who bridle their mind which travels far, moves about alone, is without a body, and hides in the chamber of the heart, will be free from the bonds of Mara (the tempter).

38. If a man's thoughts are unsteady, if he does not know the true law, if his peace of mind is troubled, his knowledge will never be perfect.

39. If a man's thoughts are not dissipated, if his mind is not perplexed, if he has ceased to think of good or evil, then there is no fear for him while he is watchful.

40. Knowing that this body is fragile like a jar, and making this thought firm like a fortress, one should attack Mara (the tempter) with the weapon of knowledge, one should watch him when conquered, and should never rest.

41. Before long, alas! this body will lie on the earth, despised, without understanding, like a useless log.

42. Whatever a hater may do to a hater, or an enemy to an enemy, a wrongly-directed mind will do us greater mischief.

43. Not a mother, not a father will do so much, nor any other relative; a well-directed mind will do us greater service.

Chapter V. The Fool

60. Long is the night to him who is awake; long is a mile to him who is tired; long is life to the foolish who do not know the true law.

61. If a traveller does not meet with one who is his better, or his equal, let him firmly keep to his solitary journey; there is no companionship with a fool.

62. 'These sons belong to me, and this wealth belongs to me,' with such thoughts a fool is tormented. He himself does not belong to himself; how much less sons and wealth?

63. The fool who knows his foolishness is wise at least so far. But a fool who thinks himself wise, he is called a fool indeed.

64. If a fool be associated with a wise man even all his life, he will perceive the truth as little as a spoon perceives the taste of soup.

65. If an intelligent man be associated for one minute only with a wise man, he will soon perceive the truth, as the tongue perceives the taste of soup.

66. Fools of little understanding have themselves for their greatest enemies, for they do evil deeds which must bear bitter fruits.

67. That deed is not well done of which a man must repent, and the reward of which he receives crying and with a tearful face.

68. No, that deed is well done of which a man does not repent, and the reward of which he receives gladly and cheerfully.

69. As long as the evil deed done does not bear fruit, the fool thinks it is like honey; but when it ripens, then the fool suffers grief.

70. Let a fool month after month eat his food like an ascetic with the tip of a blade of Kusa grass, yet he is not worth the sixteenth particle of those who have well weighed the law.

71. An evil deed, like newly-drawn milk, does not turn suddenly; smouldering, like fire covered by ashes, it follows the fool.

72. And when the evil deed, after it has become known, brings sorrow to the fool, then it destroys his bright lot, nay, it cleaves his head.

73. Let the fool wish for a false reputation, for precedence among the Bhikshus, for lordship in the convents, for worship among other people!

74. 'May both the layman and he who has left the world think that this is done by me; may they be subject to me in everything which is to be done or is not to be done,' thus is the mind of the fool, and his desire and pride increase.

75. 'One is the road that leads to wealth, another the road that leads to Nirvana'; if the Bhikshu, the disciple of Buddha, has learnt this, he will not yearn for honour, he will strive after separation from the world.

Chapter XII. Self

157. If a man hold himself dear, let him watch himself carefully; during one at least out of the three watches a wise man should be watchful.

158. Let each man direct himself first to what is proper, then let him teach others; thus a wise man will not suffer.

159. If a man make himself as he teaches others to be, then, being himself well subdued, he may subdue others; one's own self is indeed difficult to subdue.

160. Self is the lord of self, who else could be the lord? With self well subdued, a man finds a lord such as few can find.

161. The evil done by oneself, self-begotten, self-bred, crushes the foolish, as a diamond breaks a precious stone.

162. He whose wickedness is very great brings himself down to that state where his enemy wishes him to be, as a creeper does with the tree which it surrounds.

163. Bad deeds, and deeds hurtful to ourselves, are easy to do; what is beneficial and good, that is very difficult to do.

164. The foolish man who scorns the rule of the venerable (Arahat), of the elect (Ariya), of the virtuous, and follows false doctrine, he bears fruit to his own destruction, like the fruits of the Katthaka reed.

165. By oneself the evil is done, by oneself one

suffers; by oneself evil is left undone, by oneself one is purified. Purity and impurity belong to oneself, no one can purify another.

166. Let no one forget his own duty for the sake of another's, however great; let a man, after he has discerned his own duty, be always attentive to his duty.

CHAPTER XX. THE WAY

273. The best of ways is the eightfold; the best of truths the four words; the best of virtues passionlessness; the best of men he who has eyes to see.

274. This is the way, there is no other that leads to the purifying of intelligence. Go on this way! Everything else is the deceit of Mara (the tempter).

275. If you go on this way, you will make an end of pain! The way was preached by me when I had understood the removal of the thorns in the flesh.

276. You yourself must make an effort. The Tathagatas (Buddhas) are only preachers. The thoughtful who enter the way are freed from the bondage of Mara.

277. 'All created things perish', he who knows and sees this becomes passive in pain; this is the way to purity.

278. 'All created things are grief and pain', he who

knows and sees this becomes passive in pain; this is the way that leads to purity.

279. 'All forms are unreal', he who knows and sees this becomes passive in pain; this is the way that leads to purity.

280. He who does not rouse himself when it is time to rise, who, though young and strong, is full of sloth, whose will and thought are weak, that lazy and idle man will never find the way to knowledge.

281. Watching his speech, well restrained in mind, let a man never commit any wrong with his body! Let a man but keep these three roads of action clear, and he will achieve the way which is taught by the wise.

282. Through zeal knowledge is gotten, through lack of zeal knowledge is lost; let a man who knows this double path of gain and loss thus place himself that knowledge may grow.

283. Cut down the whole forest of lust, not a tree only! Danger comes out of the forest of lust. When you have cut down both the forest of lust and its undergrowth, then, Bhikshus, you will be rid of the forest and free!

284. So long as the love of man towards women, even the smallest, is not destroyed, so long is his mind in bondage, as the calf that drinks milk is to its mother.

285. Cut out the love of self, like an autumn lotus, with thy hand! Cherish the road of peace. Nirvana has been shown by Sugata (Buddha).

286. 'Here I shall dwell in the rain, here in winter

and summer,' thus the fool meditates, and does not think of his death.

287. Death comes and carries off that man, praised for his children and flocks, his mind distracted, as a flood carries off a sleeping village.

288. Sons are no help, nor a father, nor relations; there is no help from kinsfolk for one whom death has seized.

289. A wise and good man who knows the meaning of this should quickly clear the way that leads to Nirvana.

CHAPTER XXVI. THE BRAHMANA (ARHAT)

383. Stop the stream valiantly, drive away the desires, O Brahmana![1] When you have understood the destruction of all that was made, you will understand that which was not made.

384. If the Brahmana has reached the other shore in both laws (in restraint and contemplation), all bonds vanish from him who has obtained knowledge.

385. He for whom there is neither this nor that shore, nor both, him, the fearless and unshackled, I call indeed a Brahmana.

386. He who is thoughtful, blameless, settled,

1. A Brahmin, i.e. a member of the priestly caste.

dutiful, without passions, and who has attained the highest end, him I call indeed a Brahmana.

387. The sun is bright by day, the moon shines by night, the warrior is bright in his armour, the Brahmana is bright in his meditation; but Buddha, the Awakened, is bright with splendour day and night.

388. Because a man is rid of evil, therefore he is called Brahmana; because he walks quietly, therefore he is called Samana; because he has sent away his own impurities, therefore he is called Pravragita (Pabbagita, a pilgrim).

389. No one should attack a Brahmana, but no Brahmana, if attacked, should let himself fly at his aggressor! Woe to him who strikes a Brahmana, more woe to him who flies at his aggressor!

390. It advantages a Brahmana not a little if he holds his mind back from the pleasures of life; when all wish to injure has vanished, pain will cease.

391. Him I call indeed a Brahmana who does not offend by body, word, or thought, and is controlled on these three points.

392. After a man has once understood the law as taught by the Well-awakened (Buddha), let him worship it carefully, as the Brahmana worships the sacrificial fire.

393. A man does not become a Brahmana by his platted hair, by his family, or by birth; in whom there is truth and righteousness, he is blessed, he is a Brahmana.

394. What is the use of platted hair, O fool! what of the raiment of goat-skins? Within you there is ravening, but the outside you make clean.

395. The man who wears dirty raiments, who is emaciated and covered with veins, who lives alone in the forest, and meditates, him I call indeed a Brahmana.

396. I do not call a man a Brahmana because of his origin or of his mother. He is indeed arrogant, and he is wealthy: but the poor, who is free from all attachments, him I call indeed a Brahmana.

397. Him I call indeed a Brahmana who has cut all fetters, who never trembles, is independent and unshackled.

398. Him I call indeed a Brahmana who has cut the strap and the thong, the chain with all that pertains to it, who has burst the bar, and is awakened.

399. Him I call indeed a Brahmana who, though he has committed no offence, endures reproach, bonds, and stripes, who has endurance for his force, and strength for his army.

400. Him I call indeed a Brahmana who is free from anger, dutiful, virtuous, without appetite, who is subdued, and has received his last body.

401. Him I call indeed a Brahmana who does not cling to pleasures, like water on a lotus leaf, like a mustard seed on the point of a needle.

402. Him I call indeed a Brahmana who, even here, knows the end of his suffering, has put down his burden, and is unshackled.

403. Him I call indeed a Brahmana whose knowledge is deep, who possesses wisdom, who knows the right way and the wrong, and has attained the highest end.

404. Him I call indeed a Brahmana who keeps aloof both from laymen and from mendicants, who frequents no houses, and has but few desires.

405. Him I call indeed a Brahmana who finds no fault with other beings, whether feeble or strong, and does not kill nor cause slaughter.

406. Him I call indeed a Brahmana who is tolerant with the intolerant, mild with fault-finders, and free from passion among the passionate.

407. Him I call indeed a Brahmana from whom anger and hatred, pride and envy have dropped like a mustard seed from the point of a needle.

408. Him I call indeed a Brahmana who utters true speech, instructive and free from harshness, so that he offend no one.

409. Him I call indeed a Brahmana who takes nothing in the world that is not given him, be it long or short, small or large, good or bad.

410. Him I call indeed a Brahmana who fosters no desires for this world or for the next, has no inclinations, and is unshackled.

411. Him I call indeed a Brahmana who has no interests, and when he has understood the truth, does not say 'How, how?' and who has reached the depth of the Immortal.

412. Him I call indeed a Brahmana who in this

world is above good and evil, above the bondage of both, free from grief from sin, and from impurity.

413. Him I call indeed a Brahmana who is bright like the moon, pure, serene, undisturbed, and in whom all gaiety is extinct.

414. Him I call indeed a Brahmana who has traversed this miry road, the impassable world and its vanity, who has gone through, and reached the other shore, is thoughtful, guileless, free from doubts, free from attachment, and content.

415. Him I call indeed a Brahmana who in this world, leaving all desires, travels about without a home, and in whom all concupiscence is extinct.

416. Him I call indeed a Brahmana who, leaving all longings, travels about without a home, and in whom all covetousness is extinct.

417. Him I call indeed a Brahmana who, after leaving all bondage to men, has risen above all bondage to the gods, and is free from all and every bondage.

418. Him I call indeed a Brahmana who has left what gives pleasure and what gives pain, who is cold, and free from all germs (of renewed life), the hero who has conquered all the worlds.

419. Him I call indeed a Brahmana who knows the destruction and the return of beings everywhere, who is free from bondage, welfaring (Sugata), and awakened (Buddha).

420. Him I call indeed a Brahmana whose path the gods do not know, nor spirits (Gandharvas), nor men,

whose passions are extinct, and who is an Arhat (venerable).

421. Him I call indeed a Brahmana who calls nothing his own, whether it be before, behind, or between, who is poor, and free from the love of the world.

422. Him I call indeed a Brahmana, the manly, the noble, the hero, the great sage, the conqueror, the impassible, the accomplished, the awakened.

423. Him I call indeed a Brahmana who knows his former abodes, who sees heaven and hell, has reached the end of births, is perfect in knowledge, a sage, and whose perfections are all perfect.

BUDDHA, ON GOVERNANCE OF THOUGHTS

INTRODUCTION

The spiritual life begins with the inner man. It is only when the contents of the mind can be brought under some kind of control can a man orient himself with clarity towards the realities of his existence. In so doing, he obtains several benefits. He raises the general level of his being. He gains purposefulness and decision. And he communicates to others the compelling truth that he has become his own point of origin.

What is rare, even among the great spiritual classics, is practical advice on how this is to be done.

The *Vitakkasanthana Sutta*, or 'On Governance of

Thoughts', fills that gap. This discourse was given by the Buddha in a park built by one of his patrons in what is now Shravasti in Uttar Pradesh in northern India. It is a precise guide to maintaining mental and emotional equilibrium.

There are five basic techniques.

First, when unhelpful or unwholesome thoughts arise in the mind, the initial line of defence is simply to direct the mind away from those thoughts and towards helpful or wholesome thoughts; this is compared to a carpenter knocking out a rough peg and replacing it with a fine one.

Should this fail to work, the second line of defence is to consider the danger of the thoughts—where they lead and how their consequences will be unpleasant. It is intended that we are to feel disgusted and ashamed by this, and so disinclined to entertain those thoughts further.

The third technique is to avoid directing the mind towards unwanted thoughts. This requires some explanation. Obviously, it is not meant to suggest that we can simply render ourselves totally free, at one fell swoop, from troublesome thoughts—if that were possible, what need would we have for guidance in the first place? Rather, it is intended that on becoming aware of the arising of these thoughts, we are to allow them to exist but also, in turn, let them pass away—which they will do if starved of attention, whether positive or negative.

'Stilling the process of thought creating' is the

necessarily clumsy and arcane-sounding—but actually very practical and commonsensical—fourth method for dealing with unwanted thoughts. The point here is to slow down the very process by which thoughts are generated—all thoughts, helpful or unhelpful—so that the offending thoughts are frozen at the point at which (or even before) they arise. 'Just as a man who is running fast, may decide to walk slowly—or stand still—or sit down—or lie down—and thereby passes from the more violent to the easier posture—even so is it with this monk,' says the Sutta. The mind's processes *generally* are slowed down, so that the offending thoughts *specifically* can be slowed down too, and ultimately be stilled.

The final method takes a different tack. When all else has failed, it will become necessary for the monk to deal with the disobedient mind using more primitive methods: 'with his teeth clenched and with his tongue pressed against his palate, he should, by sheer force of mind, restrain, coerce, and dominate his heart.' Here we are back in familiar territory where we have to expend real energy in suppressing disobedient thoughts. 'It is as if a strong man, grabbing a weaker man by the head or the shoulders, were to hold him down, crush him, and overwhelm him.'

One insight—which is implied but not openly stated in the Sutta—is crucial. Our true nature is the pristine consciousness that with sufficient training we can deploy at will. It is *not* that jumble of half-borrowed fragmentary concepts, impressions, and prejudices that rumble around our cranial cavities. These are—to borrow a metaphor from the great Sufi poet, Jalaluddin Rumi—merely guests, and sometimes troublesome ones at that.

―――――

ON GOVERNANCE OF THOUGHTS

Thus have I heard:

Once when the Lord[1] was staying at Sāvatthī in Jeta's grove in Anāthapiṇḍika's pleasaunce, the Lord addressed the listening monks as follows.

A monk who applies himself to the higher thought should pass in review from time to time five phases of mind, and these are they:

1. When, by reason of a phase of mind, there arise in a monk bad and wrong thoughts associated with appetite, hatred, and delusion, then he should divert his mind from that to another phase associated with what is right; and, by his doing so, those bad and wrong thoughts pass away and disappear, so that his heart stands firm, is steadfast, is focussed and concentrated. Just as a skilled artisan or his apprentice will with a little peg knock and drive out and expel a big peg, so, when, by reason of a phase of mind, there

1. Buddha.

arise in a monk bad and wrong thoughts [he will be] focussed and concentrated.

2. If, though the monk diverts his mind from the former to the latter phase, there still arise in him the same bad and wrong thoughts as before, then he should study the perils these entail, marking how wrong and depraved such thoughts are and how they ripen unto ill. As he studies them, these bad and wrong thoughts pass away and disappear, so that his heart stands firm, is steadfast, is focussed and concentrated. Just as a woman or man or dressy lad, if the carcass of snake or dog or human being be slung round their necks, are filled with horror, loathing, and disgust—even so is it with this monk in his scrutiny.

3. If, for all his scrutiny of their perils, these bad and wrong thoughts still keep on arising, then he should ignore them and not let his mind dwell on them. As he ignores them, they will pass away and disappear, so that his heart stands firm, is steadfast, is focussed and concentrated. Just as a man with eyes to see, will, if he does not want to view visible forms that come within his field of vision, close his eyes or look another way—even so is it with the monk in his ignoring of bad and wrong thoughts.

4. If, for all his ignoring of them, these bad and wrong thoughts still keep on arising, then he must bethink him how to allay all that moulds and fashions thoughts. As he does so, these thoughts will pass

away and disappear, so that his heart stands firm, is steadfast, is focussed and concentrated. Just as a man who is running fast, may decide to walk slowly—or stand still—or sit down—or lie down—and thereby passes from the more violent to the easier posture—even so is it with this monk in his allaying of all that moulds and fashions thoughts.

5. But, if, allay as he may, these thoughts continue to arise, then, with his teeth clenched and with his tongue pressed against his palate, he should, by sheer force of mind, restrain, coerce, and dominate his heart. As he does so, these thoughts will pass away and disappear, so that his heart stands firm, is steadfast, is focussed and concentrated. Just as a strong man, taking a weaker man by the head or shoulders, restrains and coerces, and dominates him—even so, if, allay as he may, these thoughts [he will be] focussed and concentrated.

When at last, whether:

   1. by diverting his mind elsewhere or
   2. by scrutiny of the perilous consequences or
   3. by ignoring bad and wrong thoughts or
   4. by allaying what moulds them or
   5. by subduing them,

the monk is victorious over bad and wrong thoughts associated with appetite, hatred, and delusion, so that they pass away and disappear and his heart stands firm and is steadfast, is focussed, and concentrated—then indeed has he earned the style of master of the ordering of his thoughts, for he will think only such thoughts as he wishes and not those he wishes not to think; he has hewn away cravings, has shed his fetters, and—by fathoming propensities to pride—has made an end of ill.

Thus spoke the Lord.

Glad at heart, those monks rejoiced in what the Lord had said.

CHUANG-TZU, THE WRITINGS OF CHUANG-TZU

INTRODUCTION

Where the *Tao Te Ching* tells of the nature of the Tao and its proper employment by leaders of men, the *Writings of Chuang-tzu* tells of the personal cultivation of the Taoist sage.

The sage is, in simple terms, the supremely self-realized person who moves through the universe unruffled and unperturbed by the vicissitudes of life. Through a combination of philosophical contemplation and meditative practices, which aim to break down the distinction between self and world, the fully realized individual brings himself into harmony with the spontaneity of the Tao. He refrains from futile and counterproductive efforts to bring the world or other people under his control. Instead, he liberates himself from the artificial restraints of culture and society.

Chuang-tzu's *Writings* are not merely abstract reflections but provide concrete guidance on becoming a 'perfected' or self-realized individual.

Prominent in the *Writings* is the doctrine of 'wuwei'. *Wuwei* is 'actionless action'. It is action beyond activity—action without busy-ness, action without striving, action without friction or reactivity. *Wuwei* means following the natural 'paths of least resistance' that are laid out in the order of things: the metaphor is that of the expert cook who never attempts to chop through bones or joints but instead slides his blade through the openings and cavities that are naturally present in the animal. The Taoist sage looks to expand his awareness of these natural paths.

The Taoist sage accepts the interdependence of all things, including those that appear to stand as opposites. This can be seen in the appreciation of the often neglected subjective dimension of existence. There is both a philosophical and a practical aspect to this. Philosophically speaking, the subjective and objective dimensions of existence are intertwined and interdependent. Furthermore, practically speaking, it is often the subjective aspect of experience that is the more decisive: the best habitat, the best food, the best mates—the standards for these will all vary subjectively according to whoever it is who is making the assessment. The wisdom, foresight, and power of the Taoist sage derive to a considerable degree from this sensitivity to this subjective dimension.

The sage's ultimate achievement, however, lies in his transformation away from conventional selfhood. 'Surely the man now leaning on the table is not he who was here just now,' begins Chapter 2 of the *Writings*, which is met with the reply, '*Today I have buried myself.*' Many spiritual traditions contain within them the premise that it is necessary to die—whether metaphorically or literally or both—before we can truly live. Chuang-tzu's contribution to the theme is that the self dies and is reborn in every moment. Existence is an ongoing process of self-determination: every scintilla of time is an opportunity to start afresh.

The modern man thinks too much of his progress in the world and too little of his self-realization. The *Writings of Chuang-tzu* stands as a corrective for that tendency. The work sensitizes us to a natural order too often obscured by the rigid habits of a mechanical age. It awakens in us a capacity for appreciating the subtle nuances of things, whereby apparent opposites shade into, and reflect, one another. And it paves the way for a more spontaneous, more flexible, and more responsive approach to the questions of life and the difficulties of living.

CHAPTER 2

THE IDENTITY OF CONTRARIES

Tzŭ Ch'i of Nan-kuo sat leaning on a table. Looking up to heaven, he sighed and became absent, as though soul and body had parted. Yen Ch'êng Tzŭ Yu, who was standing by him, exclaimed, 'What are you thinking about that your body should become thus like dry wood, your mind like dead ashes? Surely the man now leaning on the table is not he who was here just now.'

'My friend,' replied Tzŭ Ch'i, 'your question is apposite. *Today I have buried myself.* ... Do you understand? ... Ah! perhaps you only know the music of Man, and not that of Earth. Or even if you have heard the music of Earth, you have not heard the music of Heaven.'

...

'There is nothing which is not objective: there is nothing which is not subjective. But it is impossible to start from the objective. Only from subjective knowledge is it possible to proceed to objective knowledge. Hence it has been said, 'The objective emanates from the subjective; the subjective is consequent upon the objective. This is the *Alternation Theory.*' Nevertheless, when one is born, the other dies. When one is possible, the other is impossible. When one is affirmative the other is negative. Which being the case, the true sage rejects

86

all distinctions of this and that. He takes his refuge in God, and places himself in subjective relation with all things.

'And inasmuch as the subjective is also objective, and the objective also subjective, and as the contraries under each are indistinguishably blended, does it not become impossible for us to say whether subjective and objective really exist at all?

'When subjective and objective are both without their correlates, that is the very axis of Tao. And when that axis passes through the centre at which all Infinities converge, positive and negative alike blend into an infinite One. Hence it has been said that there is nothing like the light of nature.'

...

'But to wear out one's intellect in an obstinate adherence to the individuality of things, not recognising the fact that all things are One—this is called *Three in the Morning*.'

'What is *Three in the Morning?*' asked Tzŭ Yu.

'A keeper of monkeys,' replied Tzŭ Ch'i, 'said with regard to their rations of chestnuts that each monkey was to have three in the morning and four at night. But at this the monkeys were very angry, so the keeper said they might have four in the morning and three at night, with which arrangement they were all well pleased. The actual number of the chestnuts remained the same, but there was an adaptation to the likes and dislikes of those concerned. Such is the principle of putting oneself into subjective relation with externals.

'Wherefore the true Sage, while regarding contraries as identical, adapts himself to the laws of Heaven. This is called following two courses at once.'

...

Yeh Ch'üeh asked Wang I, saying, 'Do you know for certain that all things are subjectively the same?'

'How can I know?' answered Wang I. 'Do you know what you do not know?'

'How can I know?' replied Yeh Ch'üeh. 'But can then nothing be known?'

'How can I know?' said Wang I. 'Nevertheless, I will try to tell you. How can it be known that what I call knowing is not really not knowing, and that what I call not knowing is not really knowing? Now I would ask you this. If a man sleeps in a damp place, he gets lumbago and dies. But how about an eel? And living up in a tree is precarious and trying to the nerves—but how about monkeys? Of the man, the eel, and the monkey, whose habitat is the right one, absolutely? Human beings feed on flesh, deer on grass, centipedes on snakes, owls and crows on mice. Of these four, whose is the right taste, absolutely? Monkey mates with monkey, the buck with the doe; eels consort with fishes, while men admire Mao Ch'iang and Li Chi, at the sight of whom fishes plunge deep down in the water, birds soar high in the air, and deer hurry away.

'Yet who shall say which is the correct standard of

beauty? In my opinion, the standard of human virtue, and of positive and negative, is so obscured that it is impossible to actually know it as such.'

...

'Those who dream of the banquet, wake to lamentation and sorrow. Those who dream of lamentation and sorrow wake to join the hunt. While they dream, they do not know that they dream. Some will even interpret the very dream they are dreaming; and only when they awake do they know it was a dream. By and by comes the Great Awakening, and then we find out that this life is really a great dream. Fools think they are awake now, and flatter themselves they know if they are really princes or peasants. Confucius and you are both dreams; and I who say you are dreams—I am but a dream myself. This is a paradox. Tomorrow a sage may arise to explain it; but that tomorrow will not be until ten thousand generations have gone by.'

...

'Granting that you and I argue. If you beat me, and not I you, are you necessarily right and I wrong? Or if I beat you and not you me, am I necessarily right and you wrong? Or are we both partly right and partly wrong? Or are we both wholly right and wholly wrong? You and I cannot know this, and consequently the world will be in ignorance of the truth.

'Who shall I employ as arbiter between us? If I employ someone who takes your view, he will side with you. How can such a one arbitrate between us? If I employ someone who takes my view, he will side with me. How can such a one arbitrate between us? And if I employ someone who either differs from, or agrees with, both of us, he will be equally unable to decide between us. Since then you, and I, and man, cannot decide, must we not depend upon another?'

...

Once upon a time, I, Chuang Tzǔ, dreamt I was a butterfly, fluttering hither and thither, to all intents and purposes a butterfly. I was conscious only of following my fancies as a butterfly, and was unconscious of my individuality as a man. Suddenly, I awaked, and there I lay, myself again. Now I do not know whether I was then a man dreaming I was a butterfly, or whether I am now a butterfly dreaming I am a man. Between a man and a butterfly there is necessarily a barrier. The transition is called *Metempsychosis*.

CHAPTER 3

COOK DING CUTS UP AN OX

My life has a limit, but my knowledge is without limit. To drive the limited in search of the limitless is fatal, and the knowledge of those who do this is fatally lost.

In striving for others, avoid fame. In striving for self, avoid disgrace. Pursue a middle course. Thus you will keep a sound body, and a sound mind, fulfil your duties, and work out your allotted span.

Prince Hui's cook was cutting up a bullock. Every blow of his hand, every heave of his shoulders, every tread of his foot, every thrust of his knee, every *whshh* of rent flesh, every *chhk* of the chopper, was in perfect harmony—rhythmical like the dance of the Mulberry Grove, simultaneous like the chords of the Ching Shou.

'Well done!' cried the Prince. 'Yours is skill indeed.'

'Sire,' replied the cook, 'I have always devoted myself to Tao. It is better than skill. When I first began to cut up bullocks, I saw before me simply *whole* bullocks. After three years' practice, I saw no more whole animals. And now I work with my mind and not with my eye. When my senses bid me stop, but my mind urges me on, I fall back upon eternal principles. I follow such openings or cavities as there may be, according to the natural constitution of the animal. I do not attempt to cut through joints; still less through large bones.

'A good cook changes his chopper once a year—because he cuts. An ordinary cook, once a month—because he hacks. But I have had this chopper nineteen years, and although I have cut up many thousand bullocks, its edge is as if fresh from the whetstone. For at the joints there are always interstices, and the edge of a chopper being without thickness, it remains only to insert that which is without thickness into such an interstice. By these means, the interstice will be enlarged, and the blade will find plenty of room. It is thus that I have kept my chopper for nineteen years as though fresh from the whetstone.

'Nevertheless, when I come upon a hard part where the blade meets with a difficulty, I am all caution. I fix my eye on it. I stay my hand, and gently apply my blade, until with a *hwah* the part yields like earth crumbling to the ground. Then I take out my chopper, and stand up, and look around, and pause, until with an air of triumph I wipe my chopper and put it carefully away.'

'Bravo!' cried the Prince. 'From the words of this cook I have learnt how to take care of my life.'

CHAPTER 4

A USELESS TREE

A certain artisan was travelling to the Ch'i State. On reaching Ch'ü-yüan, he saw a sacred *li* tree, large enough to hide an ox behind it, a hundred spans in girth, towering up ten cubits over the hilltop, and carrying behind it branches, many tens of the smallest of which were of a size for boats. Crowds stood gazing at it, but our artisan took no notice, and went on his way without even casting a look behind. His apprentice, however, gazed his fill, and when he caught up his master, said, 'Ever since I have handled an adze in your service, I have never seen such a splendid piece of timber as that. How was it that you, sir, did not care to stop and look at it?'

'It's not worth talking about,' replied his master. 'It's good for nothing. Make a boat of it—'twould sink. A coffin—'twould rot. Furniture—'twould soon break down. A door—'twould sweat. A pillar—'twould be worm-eaten. It is wood of no quality, and of no use. That is why it has attained its present age.'

When the artisan reached home, he dreamt that the tree appeared to him in a dream and spoke as follows: 'What is it that you compare me with? Is it with the more elegant trees? The cherry-apple, the pear, the orange, the pomelo, and other fruit-bearers, as soon as their fruit ripens are stripped and treated with indignity. The great boughs are snapped off, the small ones scattered abroad. Thus do these trees by their own value injure their own lives. They cannot fulfil their allotted span of years, but perish prematurely in mid-career from their entanglement with the world around them. Thus it is with all things. For a long period, my aim was to be useless. Many times I was in danger, but at length I succeeded, and so became useful as I am today. But had I then been of use, I should not now be of the great use I am. Moreover, you and I belong both to the same category of things. Have done then with this criticism of others. Is a good-for-nothing fellow whose dangers are not yet passed a fit person to talk of a good-for-nothing tree?'

When our artisan awoke and told his dream, his apprentice said, 'If the tree aimed at uselessness, how was it that it became a sacred tree?'

'What you don't understand,' replied his master, 'don't talk about. That was merely to escape from the attacks of its enemies. Had it not become sacred, how many would have wanted to cut it down! The means of safety adopted were different from ordinary means, and to test these by ordinary canons leaves one far wide of the mark.'

Tzŭ Ch'i of Nan-poh was travelling on the Shang mountain when he saw a large tree which astonished him very much. A thousand chariot teams could have found shelter under its shade.

'What tree is this?' cried Tzŭ Ch'i. 'Surely it must have unusually fine timber.' Then looking up, he saw that its branches were too crooked for rafters; while as to the trunk he saw that its irregular grain made it valueless for coffins. He tasted a leaf, but it took the skin off his lips, and its odour was so strong that it would make a man as it were drunk for three days together.

'Ah!' said Tzŭ Ch'i. 'This tree is good for nothing, and that is how it has attained this size. A wise man might well follow its example.'

CHAPTER 18

AN EMPTY SKULL

Chuang Tzŭ one day saw an empty skull, bleached, but still preserving its shape. Striking it with his riding whip, he said, 'Were you once some ambitious citizen whose inordinate yearnings brought him to this pass?—some statesman who plunged his country in ruin and perished in the fray?—some wretch who left behind him a legacy of shame?—some beggar who died in the pangs of hunger and cold? Or did you reach this state by the natural course of old age?'

When he had finished speaking, he took the skull, and placing it under his head as a pillow, went to sleep. In the night, he dreamt that the skull appeared to him and said, 'You speak well, sir; but all you say has reference to the life of mortals, and to mortal troubles. In death there are none of these. Would you like to hear about death?'

Chuang Tzŭ having replied in the affirmative, the skull began: 'In death, there is no sovereign above, and no subject below. The workings of the four seasons are unknown. Our existences are bounded only by eternity. The happiness of a king among men cannot exceed that which we enjoy.'

Chuang Tzŭ, however, was not convinced, and said, 'Were I to prevail upon God to allow your body to be born again, and your bones and flesh to be renewed, so that you could return to your parents, to your wife, and to the friends of your youth—would you be willing?'

At this, the skull opened its eyes wide and knitted its brows and said, 'How should I cast aside happiness greater than that of a king, and mingle once again in the toils and troubles of mortality?'

CHAPTER 19

THE OBLITERATION OF SELF

Ch'ing, the chief carpenter of the Lu State, was carving wood into a stand for hanging musical instruments. When finished, the work appeared to those who saw it as though of supernatural execution. And the prince of Lu asked him, saying, 'What mystery is there in your art?'

'No mystery, your Highness,' replied Ch'ing, 'and yet there is something. When I am about to make such a stand, I guard against any diminution of my vital power. I first reduce my mind to absolute quiescence. Three days in this condition, and I become oblivious of any reward to be gained. Five days, and I become oblivious of any fame to be acquired. Seven days, and I become unconscious of my four limbs and my physical frame. Then, with no thought of the court present to my mind, my skill becomes concentrated, and all disturbing elements from without are gone. I enter some mountain forest.

I search for a suitable tree. It contains the form required, which is afterwards elaborated. I see the stand in my mind's eye, and then set to work. Otherwise, there is nothing. I bring my own natural capacity into relation with that of the wood. What was suspected to be of supernatural execution in my work was due solely to this.'

CHAPTER 20

TWO CONCUBINES

When Yang Tzŭ went to the Sung State, he passed a night at an inn. The innkeeper had two concubines, one beautiful, the other ugly. The latter he loved; the former, he hated. Yang Tzŭ asked how this was; whereupon one of the inn servants said, 'The beautiful one is so conscious of her beauty that one does not think her beautiful. The ugly one is so conscious of her ugliness that one does not think her ugly.'

'Note this, my disciples!' cried Yang Tzŭ. 'Be virtuous, but without being consciously so; and wherever you go, you will be beloved.'

HUAINANZI, THE OLD MAN WHO LOST HIS HORSE

INTRODUCTION

A man loses his horse. He is commiserated. Months later the horse returns bringing a fine nomad horse with it. He is congratulated. The man's son, who liked to ride, falls from one of the horses and breaks his leg. He is commiserated. Then the nomads raid the area, killing nine out of ten of the young men who took up arms against them. The man's son survives—his father had kept him back from battle because he was lame.

This short yet powerful story comes from the *Huainanzi*, an ancient Chinese collection of essays resulting from debates held at the court of Liu An, King of Huainan, in the second century BC.

Each of us will be able to identify similar patterns of events in our own lives. Looking back, we can often see how one event, which we experienced at the time as a setback, led to another event that we experienced at the time as a triumph, which led in turn to a further event experienced as a setback, and so on. In a sense, it has to be this way: our lives are inevitably built upon what went before, so that subsequent downturns and upturns can always be traced back to choices we have made previously. It is because we experience life as a kind of eternal present, however, that we cannot anticipate the bad that comes from good and the good that comes from bad. But we can always see it in retrospect.

The story, short as it is, in many ways encapsulates in miniature many of the themes of the spiritual path we have been exploring. There's human incomprehension in the face of universal plan—that's what we have seen in Ecclesiastes. There's the virtue of inaction—actionless action—that we have seen in the *Tao Te Ching*. There is the perspectivism that we have seen in Chuang-tzu. There is the mental composure we see advocated in the Buddhist texts and the non-attachment doctrine we will see in the *Bhagavad Gita*. In fact, the story of the old man who lost his horse communicates what is probably the central insight of all the spiritual traditions—that there is a providential order in the universe which can occasionally be glimpsed but never fully understood.

THE OLD MAN WHO LOST HIS HORSE (SAI WENG SHI MA)

There was a father, well versed in the workings of fate, who lived close to the frontier with his son. One of the father's horses accidentally strayed across the border into the land of the nomads. Everyone else commiserated with him, but the father said, 'How do you know this won't turn out to be good luck?'

After several months, the horse returned from the land of the nomads, accompanied by another fine horse. Everyone else congratulated him, but the father said, 'How do you know this won't turn out to be bad luck?'

The family was rich in fine horses, and the man's son loved riding them. One day the son fell and broke his leg, so everyone commiserated with him, but the father said, 'How do you know this won't turn out to be good luck?'

One year later, the nomads invaded the frontier, and all able-bodied men took up arms and went to do battle. Of the men who lived near the frontier, nine out of ten died. The father and son were only spared from this tragedy because of the son's broken leg.

Thus good fortune turning into misfortune and

misfortune turning into good fortune goes on without end, and the depths of it cannot be penetrated.

8

BHAGAVAD GITA

INTRODUCTION

Take yourself to a battlefield in northern India many centuries back in the pre-Christian era. There has been a conflict over succession to the throne between two groups of cousins, the Pandavas and the Kauravas. The Pandavas have been denied their share of the kingdom and now line up on the battlefield facing the opposing army of the Kauravas. The battle, which has not yet begun, will rage for eighteen days and result in defeat and death of all the Kauravas. Only the five Pandava brothers and Krishna (who has been acting as their counsellor) survive. Thereafter, all except one of those brothers die too.

In circumstances such as these, how is a man to act?

This is the question posed by the *Bhagavad Gita*, a dialogue from the larger *Mahabharata*, that occurs between Arjuna (hero of the Pandavas) and Krishna (incarnation of the Godhead) who has been acting as his charioteer. Arjuna has pulled up his chariot and refused to proceed: he is a warrior and it is his duty to fight, but those whom he is tasked to kill are blood relatives deserving of respect and veneration. This is Krishna's moment to speak—not just to Arjuna but, through the *Gita* itself, to all mankind.

Krishna talks first of the *dharma*—the moral law that governs the universe. *Dharma* is 'what is right'. This is different for every man. It differs according to a man's *varna* or 'caste'. It also differs for every individual, since each man's nature is unique. For a member of the warrior caste, like Arjuna, *dharma* means measuring up to one's own highest nature as a hero capable of acting without hesitation on the field of battle. It carries with it a duty to fight and kill without surrendering to any impulse for self-preservation.

Krishna also talks of yoga. Yoga in this context refers to union with the absolute as well as the exercises and techniques necessary to realize that union. Specifically, the *Gita* makes reference to a path of yoga known as karma yoga premised upon the necessity of taking action in the world without any attachment to the work or desire for its results. 'Your business is with action alone,' tells Krishna, 'not by any means with fruit.' Be equable in success or ill-success, he advises; those whose motive to action is the 'fruit' of action are wretched.

And Krishna talks of war. Given that the *Gita* is

104

a spiritual classic, it is not surprising that several commentators have focussed on war as an allegory of the 'war within'. War represents the struggle for self-mastery, it is said, that we all must undergo in order to emerge from life victorious. Be that as it may, it is undoubtedly not the whole story. The *Gita* is a resolute defence and justification of the warrior's duty to conduct actual war when called upon to do so. It is a spirited call to action to confront not only our inner demons, but those that come at us from the outside too.

For the modern man, the *Gita* represents a kind of spirituality that is seen and reflected upon far too rarely. It demonstrates in no uncertain terms that the spiritual path can be bold, brave, noble, and active. Gandhi referred to the *Gita* as his 'spiritual dictionary'. 'I find a solace in the *Bhagavad Gita* that I miss even in the Sermon on the Mount,' he said. 'When disappointment stares me in the face and all alone I see not one ray of light, I go back to the *Bhagavad Gita*. I find a verse here and a verse there and I immediately begin to smile in the midst of overwhelming tragedies—and my life has been full of external tragedies—if they have left no visible, no indelible scar on me, I owe it all to the teaching of *Bhagavad Gita*.' If it helped one frail old man to change the course of his nation's history, there's every reason to think it can serve as a source of strength for men of the present times, and men of the future, as they begin to awaken to their own respective missions.

———

CHAPTER II

Sanjaya[1] said:

To him,[2] who was thus overcome with pity, and dejected, and whose eyes were full of tears and turbid, the destroyer of Madhu[3] spoke these words.

The Deity[4] said:

How comes it that this delusion, O Arjuna, which is discarded by the good, which excludes from heaven, and occasions infamy, has overtaken you in this place of peril? Be not effeminate, O son of Pritha,[5] it is not worthy of you. Cast off this base weakness of heart, and arise, O terror of your foes!

Arjuna said:

How, O destroyer of Madhu, shall I encounter with arrows in the battle Bhishma[6] and Drona[7]—both, O

---

1. Sanjaya is secretary to the blind King Dhritarashtra and narrates the battle to him.
2. Arjuna.
3. Krishna.
4. Krishna.
5. Arjuna's mother.
6. Supreme commander of the Kaurava forces but related to both the Pandavas and Kauravas.
7. Supreme commander of the Kaurava forces after the fall of Bhishma, he had been preceptor to both Pandavas and Kauravas.

destroyer of enemies, entitled to reverence—without killing my preceptors—men of great glory? It is better to live even on alms in this world. But if killing them, though they are avaricious of worldly goods, I should only enjoy blood-tainted enjoyments. Nor do we know which of the two is better for us—whether that we should vanquish them, or that they should vanquish us. Even those, whom having killed, we do not wish to live—even those sons of Dhritarashtra stand arrayed against us. With a heart contaminated by the taint of helplessness, with a mind confounded about my duty, I ask you. Tell me what is assuredly good for me. I am your disciple; instruct me, who have thrown myself on your indulgence. For I do not perceive what is to dispel that grief which will dry up my organs after I shall have obtained a prosperous kingdom on earth without a foe, or even the sovereignty of the gods.

Sanjaya said:

Having spoken thus to Hrishikesa,[8] O terror of your foes, Gudakesa[9] said to Govinda,[10] 'I shall not engage in battle', and verily remained silent. To him thus desponding between the two armies, O descendant of Bharata,[11] Hrishikesa spoke these words with a slight smile.

The Deity said:

8. Krishna.
9. Arjuna.
10. Krishna.
11. Ancestor of the Pandavas and Kauravas.

You have grieved for those who deserve no grief, and you speak words of wisdom. Learned men grieve not for the living nor the dead. Never did I not exist, nor you, nor these rulers of men; nor will any one of us ever hereafter cease to be. As in this body, infancy and youth and old age come to the embodied self, so does the acquisition of another body; a sensible man is not deceived about that. The contacts of the senses, O son of Kunti,[12] which produce cold and heat, pleasure and pain, are not permanent, they are forever coming and going. Bear them, O descendant of Bharata! For, O chief of men, that sensible man whom they afflict not, pain and pleasure being alike to him, he merits immortality. There is no existence for that which is unreal; there is no non-existence for that which is real. And the correct conclusion about both is perceived by those who perceive the truth. Know that to be indestructible which pervades all this; the destruction of that inexhaustible principle none can bring about. These bodies appertaining to the embodied self which is eternal, indestructible, and indefinable, are declared to be perishable; therefore do engage in battle, O descendant of Bharata! He who thinks one to be the killer and he who thinks one to be killed, both know nothing. He kills not, is not killed. He is not born, nor does he ever die, nor, having existed, does he exist no more. Unborn, everlasting, unchangeable, and very ancient, he is not

12. Arjuna's mother.

108

killed when the body is killed. O son of Pritha, how can that man who knows the self thus to be indestructible, everlasting, unborn, and imperishable, kill anyone, or cause anyone to be killed? As a man, casting off old clothes, puts on others and new ones, so the embodied self, casting off old bodies, goes to others and new ones. Weapons do not divide the self into pieces; fire does not burn it; waters do not moisten it; the wind does not dry it up. It is not divisible; it is not combustible; it is not to be moistened; it is not to be dried up. It is everlasting, all-pervading, stable, firm, and eternal. It is said to be unperceived, to be unthinkable, to be unchangeable. Therefore knowing it to be such, you ought not to grieve. But even if you think that the self is constantly born, and constantly dies, still, O you of mighty arms, you ought not to grieve thus. For to one that is born, death is certain; and to one that dies, birth is certain. Therefore about this unavoidable thing, you ought not to grieve. The source of things, O descendant of Bharata, is unperceived; their middle state is perceived; and their end again is unperceived. What occasion is there for any lamentation regarding them? One looks upon it as a wonder; another similarly speaks of it as a wonder; another too hears of it as a wonder; and even after having heard of it, no one does really know it. This embodied self, O descendant of Bharata, within everyone's body is ever indestructible. Therefore you ought not to grieve for any being. Having regard to your own duty also, you ought not to falter, for there is nothing better for a Kshatriya[13] than a righteous battle. Happy those Kshatriyas, O son of Pritha, who can find such a battle to fight—come of itself—an open door to heaven! But if you will not fight this righteous battle, then you will have abandoned your own duty and your fame, and you will incur sin. All beings, too, will tell of your everlasting infamy; and to one who has been honoured, infamy is a greater evil than death. Warriors who are masters of great cars will think that you abstained from the battle through fear, and having been highly thought of by them, you will fall down to littleness. Your enemies, too, decrying your power, will speak much about you that should not be spoken. And what, indeed, more lamentable than that? Killed, you will obtain heaven; victorious, you will enjoy the earth. Therefore arise, O son of Kunti, resolved to engage in battle. Looking on pleasure and pain, on gain and loss, on victory and defeat as the same, prepare for battle, and thus you will not incur sin. The knowledge here declared to you is that relating to the Sankhya.[14] Now hear that relating to the Yoga. Possessed of this knowledge, O son of Pritha, you will cast off the bonds of action. In this path to final emancipation nothing that is commenced becomes abortive; no obstacles exist; and even a little of this form of piety protects one from

13. A member of the warrior caste.
14. A philosophy teaching salvation through knowledge of the dualism of matter and souls.

great danger. There is here, O descendant of Kuru, but one state of mind consisting in firm understanding. But the states of mind of those who have no firm understanding are manifold and endless. The state of mind which consists in firm understanding regarding steady contemplation does not belong to those, O son of Pritha, who are strongly attached to worldly pleasures and power, and whose minds are drawn away by that flowery talk which is full of the ordinances of specific acts for the attainment of those pleasures and that power, and which promises birth as the fruit of acts—that flowery talk which those unwise ones utter, who are enamoured of Vedic words, who say there is nothing else, who are full of desires, and whose goal is heaven. The Vedas[15] merely relate to the effects of the three qualities; do you, O Arjuna, rise above those effects of the three qualities, and be free from the pairs of opposites, always preserve courage, be free from anxiety for new acquisitions or protection of old acquisitions, and be self-controlled. To the instructed Brahmana, there is in all the Vedas as much utility as in a reservoir of water into which waters flow from all sides. Your business is with action alone; not by any means with fruit. Let not the fruit of action be your motive to action. Let not your attachment be fixed on inaction. Having recourse to devotion, O Dhanangaya,[16] perform actions, casting off all

15. The original Sanskrit texts of India's ancient spiritual culture.

attachment, and being equable in success or ill-success; such equability is called devotion. Action, O Dhanangaya, is far inferior to the devotion of the mind. In that devotion seek shelter. Wretched are those whose motive to action is the fruit of action. He who has obtained devotion in this world casts off both merit and sin. Therefore apply yourself to devotion; devotion in all actions is wisdom. The wise who have obtained devotion cast off the fruit of action; and released from the shackles of repeated births, repair to that seat where there is no unhappiness. When your mind shall have crossed beyond the taint of delusion, then will you become indifferent to all that you have heard or will hear. When your mind, that was confounded by what you have heard, will stand firm and steady in contemplation, then will you acquire devotion.

Arjuna said:

What are the characteristics, O Kesava,[17] of one whose mind is steady, and who is intent on contemplation? How should one of a steady mind speak, how sit, how move?

The Deity said:

When a man, O son of Pritha, abandons all the desires of his heart, and is pleased in his self only and by his self, he is then called of a steady mind. He whose heart is not agitated in the midst of calamities,

16. Arjuna.
17. A name for Vishnu, the god of whom Krishna is an avatar.

who has no longing for pleasures, and from whom the feelings of affection, fear, and wrath have departed, is called a sage of a steady mind. His mind is steady, who, being without attachments anywhere, feels no exultation and no aversion on encountering the various agreeable and disagreeable things of this world. A man's mind is steady, when he withdraws his senses from all objects of sense, as the tortoise withdraws its limbs from all sides. Objects of sense withdraw themselves from a person who is abstinent; not so the taste for those objects. But even the taste departs from him, when he has seen the Supreme. The boisterous senses, O son of Kunti, carry away by force the mind even of a wise man, who exerts himself for final emancipation. Restraining them all, a man should remain engaged in devotion, making me his only resort. For his mind is steady whose senses are under his control. The man who ponders over objects of sense forms an attachment to them; from that attachment is produced desire; and from desire anger is produced; from anger results want of discrimination; from want of discrimination, confusion of the memory; from confusion of the memory, loss of reason; and in consequence of loss of reason he is utterly ruined. But the self-restrained man who moves among objects with senses under the control of his own self, and free from affection and aversion, obtains tranquillity. When there is tranquillity, all his miseries are destroyed, for the mind of him whose heart is tranquil soon becomes steady. He who is not self-restrained has no steadiness of mind; nor has he who is not self-restrained perseverance in the pursuit of self-knowledge; there is no tranquility for him who does not persevere in the pursuit of self-knowledge; and whence can there be happiness for one who is not tranquil? For the heart which follows the rambling senses leads away his judgment, as the wind leads a boat astray upon the waters. Therefore, O you of mighty arms, his mind is steady whose senses are restrained on all sides from objects of sense. The self-restrained man is awake when it is night for all beings; and when all beings are awake, that is the night of the right-seeing sage. He into whom all objects of desire enter, as waters enter the ocean, which, though replenished, still keeps its position unmoved—he only obtains tranquility; not he who desires those objects of desire. The man who, casting off all desires, lives free from attachments, who is free from egoism, and from the feeling that this or that is mine, obtains tranquility. This, O son of Pritha, is the Brahmic state; attaining to this, one is never deluded; and remaining in it in one's last moments, one attains Brahma-nirvana, the Brahmic bliss.

AL-GHAZALI, THE ALCHEMY OF HAPPINESS

INTRODUCTION

One of the most profound and intriguing of the spiritual traditions is the mystical dimension of Islam known as Sufism.

Of the great Sufi figures, few are considered the equal of Abu Hamid Muhammad ibn Muhammad al-Ghazali, now known in Arabic and English as simply 'al-Ghazali'. Al-Ghazali was a Persian philosopher, theologian, and mystic. Having been appointed Professor of Theology at Baghdad at the age of only thirty-three, he was soon gripped by a spiritual crisis. He abandoned his career, disposed of his wealth, and went into life in seclusion as a Sufi mystic. He went on to make Sufism an acceptable part of orthodox Islam.

Islam can be understood as having three dimensions. The first dimension is the one most widely known to outsiders: it is the dimension from which the faith takes its name, 'submission' (*islam*), which corresponds to the 'Five Pillars'—the testimony of faith, the daily prayers, the alms tax, fasting during Ramadan, and pilgrimage to Mecca. The second dimension is 'faith' (*imam*) and refers to belief in the theological teachings. The third and lesser-known dimension is 'doing the beautiful' (*ihsan*). It is 'doing the beautiful' that the Sufis have taken as their own special domain.

The Sufi way of 'doing the beautiful' means teaching people how to transform themselves so as to come into harmony with the divine ground of being. The starting point is learning to perceive God's presence throughout the world as well as in the self. It involves the realization that we are primarily spiritual beings whose greatest happiness is to be found in personal experience of identity with ultimate reality. It also involves living in full awareness that the self is engaged at all times in a process of never-ending self-renewal, making the Sufi a 'child of the moment'. And it involves cultivating onself so as to actualize divine character traits latent in the soul.

Al-Ghazali's *Alchemy of Happiness* serves as a guide for self-transformation. The core of this transformation, for al-Ghazali, is the application of moral discipline which 'purifies the heart from the rust of passion and resentment' until 'like a clear mirror, it reflects the light of God'. Doing this will have two profound effects. First, by opening the inner being to a deeper dimension of reality, the believer will become more sensitive to meaningful impressions and intuitions. And second, mastery of self is the first step to taking control of the outside world: those souls that are able to exercise self-control will also be better able to influence others.

Sufism has been called 'an adventure in living'. For the Sufi, the world is a 'fashioning instrument': we become who we become as a result of the many impacts upon us from the outside world and what we have been able to make of them; personality is the product of the interaction between these impacts and the mind itself. What makes the Sufis special is that they engage in this process consciously. This is the 'alchemy' of which the mystics talk and which renders the Sufi more potent and effectual because more intimately attuned to the true nature of being.

CHAPTER I

THE KNOWLEDGE OF SELF

Knowledge of self is the key to the knowledge of God, according to the saying: 'He who knows himself knows God', and, as it is written in the Koran, 'We will show them Our signs in the world and *in themselves*, that the truth may be manifest to them.' Now nothing is nearer to you than yourself, and if you know not yourself how can you know anything else? If you say 'I know myself', meaning your outward shape, body, face, limbs, and so forth, such knowledge can never be a key to the knowledge of God. Nor, if your knowledge as to that which is within only extends so far, that when you are hungry you eat, and when you are angry you attack someone, will you progress any further in this path, for the beasts are your partners in this. But real self-knowledge consists in knowing the following things: What are you in yourself, and from whence have you come? Where are you going, and for what purpose have you come to tarry here awhile, and in what does your real happiness and misery consist? Some of your attributes are those of animals, some of devils, and some of angels, and you have to find out which of these attributes are accidental and which essential. Till you know this, you cannot find out where your real happiness lies. The occupation of animals is eating, sleeping, and fighting; therefore, if you are an animal, busy yourself in these things. Devils are busy in stirring up mischief, and in guile and deceit; if you belong to them, do their work. Angels contemplate the beauty of God, and are entirely free from animal qualities; if you are of angelic nature, then strive towards your origin, that you may know and contemplate the Most High, and be delivered from the thraldom of lust and anger. You should also discover why you have been created with these two animal instincts: whether they should subdue and lead you captive, or whether you should subdue them, and, in your upward progress, make of one your steed and of the other your weapon.

The first step to self-knowledge is to know that you are composed of an outward shape, called the body, and an inward entity called the heart, or soul. By 'heart', I do not mean the piece of flesh situated in the left of our bodies, but that which uses all the other faculties as its instruments and servants. In truth it does not belong to the visible world, but to the invisible, and has come into this world as a traveller visits a foreign country for the sake of merchandise, and will presently return to its native land. It is the knowledge of this entity and its attributes which is the key to the knowledge of God.

Some idea of the reality of the heart, or spirit, may be obtained by a man closing his eyes and forgetting everything around except his individuality. He will thus also obtain a glimpse of the unending nature of that individuality. Too close inquiry, however, into the essence of spirit is forbidden by the Law. In the Koran it is written: 'They will question thee concerning the spirit. Say: "The Spirit comes by the command of my Lord."' Thus much is known of it that it is an indivisible essence belonging to the world of decrees, and that it is not from everlasting, but created. An exact philosophical knowledge of the spirit is not a necessary preliminary to walking in the path of religion, but comes rather as the result of self-discipline and perseverance in that path, as it is said in the Koran: 'Those who strive in our way, verily we will guide them to the right paths.'

For the carrying on of this spiritual warfare by which the knowledge of oneself and of God is to be obtained, the body may be figured as a kingdom, the soul as its king, and the different senses and faculties as constituting an army. Reason may be called the vizier, or prime minister, passion the revenue-collector, and anger the police-officer. Under the guise of collecting revenue, passion is continually prone to plunder on its own account, while resentment is always inclined to harshness and extreme severity. Both of these, the revenue-collector and the police-officer, have to be kept in due subordination to the king, but not killed or expelled, as they have their own proper functions to fulfil. But if passion and resentment master reason, the ruin of the soul infallibly ensues. A soul which allows its lower faculties to dominate the higher is as one who should hand over an angel to the power of a dog or a Mussalman[1] to the tyranny of an unbeliever. The cultivation of demonic, animal, or angelic qualities results in the production of corresponding characters, which in the Day of Judgment will be

1. Muslim.

manifested in visible shapes, the sensual appearing as swine, the ferocious as dogs and wolves, and the pure as angels. The aim of moral discipline is to purify the heart from the rust of passion and resentment, till, like a clear mirror, it reflects the light of God.

Someone may here object, 'But if man has been created with animal and demonic qualities as well as angelic, how are we to know that the latter constitute his real essence, while the former are merely accidental and transitory?' To this I answer that the essence of each creature is to be sought in that which is highest in it and peculiar to it. Thus the horse and the ass are both burden-bearing animals, but the superiority of the horse to the ass consists in its being adapted for use in battle. If it fails in this, it becomes degraded to the rank of burden-bearing animals. Similarly with man: the highest faculty in him is reason, which fits him for the contemplation of God. If this predominates in him, when he dies, he leaves behind him all tendencies to passion and resentment, and becomes capable of association with angels. As regards his mere animal qualities, man is inferior to many animals, but reason makes him superior to them, as it is written in the Koran: 'To man we have subjected all things in the earth.' But if his lower tendencies have triumphed, after death he will ever be looking towards the earth and longing for earthly delights.

Now the rational soul in man abounds in, marvels, both of knowledge and power. By means of it he masters arts and sciences, can pass in a flash from earth to heaven and back again, can map out the skies and measure the distances between the stars. By it also he can draw the fish from the sea and the birds from the air, and can subdue to his service animals, like the elephant, the camel, and the horse. His five senses are like five doors opening on the external world; but, more wonderful than this, his heart has a window which opens on the unseen world of spirits. In the state of sleep, when the avenues of the senses are closed, this window is opened and man receives impressions from the unseen world and sometimes foreshadowings of the future. His heart is then like a mirror which reflects what is pictured in the Tablet of Fate. But, even in sleep, thoughts of worldly things dull this mirror, so, that the impressions it receives are not clear. After death, however, such thoughts vanish and things are seen in their naked reality, and the saying in the Koran is fulfilled: 'We have stripped the veil from off you and your sight today is keen.'

This opening of a window in the heart towards the unseen also takes place in conditions approaching those of prophetic inspiration, when intuitions spring up in the mind unconveyed through any sense-channel. The more a man purifies himself from fleshly lusts and concentrates his mind on God, the more conscious will he be of such intuitions. Those who are not conscious of them have no right to deny their reality.

Nor are such intuitions confined only to those of

prophetic rank. Just as iron, by sufficient polishing, can be made into a mirror, so any mind by due discipline can be rendered receptive of such impressions. It was at this truth the Prophet hinted when he said, 'Every child is born with a predisposition towards Islam; then his parents make a Jew, or a Christian, or a star-worshipper of him.' Every human being has in the depths of his consciousness heard the question 'Am I not your Lord?' and answered 'Yes' to it. But some hearts are like mirrors so befouled with rust and dirt that they give no clear reflections, while those of the prophets and saints, though they are men 'of like passions with us', are extremely sensitive to all divine impressions.

Nor is it only by reason of knowledge acquired and intuitive that the soul of man holds the first rank among created things, but also by reason of power. Just as angels preside over the elements, so does the soul rule the members of the body. Those souls which attain a special degree of power not only rule their own body but those of others also. If they wish a sick man to recover he recovers, or a person in health to fall ill he becomes ill, or if they will the presence of a person he comes to them. According as the effects produced by these powerful souls are good or bad they are termed miracles or sorceries. These souls differ from common folk in three ways: (1) what others only see in dreams they see in their waking moments; (2) while others' wills only affect their own bodies, these, by willpower, can move bodies

123

extraneous to themselves; (3) the knowledge which others acquire by laborious learning comes to them by intuition.

These three, of course, are not the only marks which differentiate them from common people, but the only ones that come within our cognisance. Just as no one knows the real nature of God but God Himself, so no one knows the real nature of a prophet but a prophet. Nor is this to be wondered at, as in everyday matters we see that it is impossible to explain the charm of poetry to one whose ear is insusceptible of cadence and rhythm, or the glories of colour to one who is stone-blind. Besides mere incapacity, there are other hindrances to the attainment of spiritual truth. One of these is externally acquired knowledge. To use a figure, the heart may be represented as a well, and the five senses as five streams which are continually conveying water to it. In order to find out the real contents of the heart these streams must be stopped for a time, at any rate, and the refuse they have brought with them must be cleared out of the well. In other words, if we are to arrive at pure spiritual truth, we must put away, for the time, knowledge which has been acquired by external processes and which too often hardens into dogmatic prejudice.

A mistake of an opposite kind is made by shallow people who, echoing some phrases which they have caught from Sufi teachers, go about decrying all knowledge. This is as if a person who was not an adept in alchemy were to go about saying, 'Alchemy is better than in gold', and were to refuse gold when it was offered to him. Alchemy *is* better than gold, but real alchemists are very rare, and so are real Sufis. He who has a mere smattering of Sufism is not superior to a learned man, any more than he who has tried a few experiments in alchemy has ground for despising a rich man.

Anyone who will look into the matter will see that happiness is necessarily linked with the knowledge of God. Each faculty of ours delights in that for which it was created: lust delights in accomplishing desire, anger in taking vengeance, the eye in seeing beautiful objects, and the ear in hearing harmonious sounds. The highest function of the soul of man is the perception of truth; in this accordingly it finds its special delight. Even in trifling matters, such as learning chess, this holds good, and the higher the subject-matter of the knowledge obtained the greater the delight. A man would be pleased at being admitted into the confidence of a prime minister, but how much more if the king makes an intimate of him and discloses state secrets to him!

An astronomer who, by his knowledge, can map the stars and describe their courses, derives more pleasure from his knowledge than the chess player from his. Seeing, then, that nothing is higher than God, how great must be the delight which springs from the true knowledge of Him!

A person in whom the desire for this knowledge

has disappeared is like one who has lost his appetite for healthy food, or who prefers feeding on clay to eating bread. All bodily appetites perish at death with the organs they use, but the soul dies not, and retains whatever knowledge of God it possesses; nay, increases it.

An important part of our knowledge of God arises from the study and contemplation of our own bodies, which reveal to us the power, wisdom, and love of the Creator. His power, in that from a mere drop He has built up the wonderful frame of man; His wisdom is revealed in its intricacies and the mutual adaptability of its parts; and His love is shown by His not only supplying such organs as are absolutely necessary for existence, as the liver, the heart, and the brain, but those which are not absolutely necessary, as the hand, the foot, the tongue, and the eye. To these He has added, as ornaments, the blackness of the hair, the redness of lips, and the curve of the eyebrows.

Man has been truly termed a 'microcosm', or little world in himself, and the structure of his body should be studied not only by those who wish to become doctors, but by those who wish to attain to a more intimate knowledge of God, just as close study of the niceties and shades of language in a great poem reveals to us more and more of the genius of its author.

But, when all is said, the knowledge of the soul plays a more important part in leading to the knowledge of God than the knowledge of our body and its functions. The body may be compared to a steed and the soul to its rider; the body was created for the soul, the soul for the body. If a man knows not his own soul, which is the nearest thing to him, what is the use of his claiming to know others? It is as if a beggar who has not the wherewithal for a meal should claim to be able to feed a town.

In this chapter we have attempted, in some degree, to expound the greatness of man's soul. He who neglects it and suffers its capacities to rust or to degenerate must necessarily be the loser in this world and the next. The true greatness of man lies in his capacity for eternal progress, otherwise in this temporal sphere he is the weakest of all things, being subject to hunger, thirst, heat, cold, and sorrow. Those things he takes most delight in are often the most injurious to him, and those things which benefit him are not to be obtained without toil and trouble. As to his intellect, a slight disarrangement of matter in his brain is sufficient to destroy or madden him; as to his power, the sting of a wasp is sufficient to rob him of ease and sleep; as to his temper, he is upset by the loss of a sixpence; as to his beauty, he is little more than nauseous matter covered with a fair skin. Without frequent washing he becomes utterly repulsive and disgraceful.

In truth, man in this world is extremely weak and contemptible; it is only in the next that he will be of value, if by means of the 'alchemy of happiness' he rises from the rank of beasts to that of angels.

Otherwise his condition will be worse than the brutes, which perish and turn to dust. It is necessary for him, at the same time that he is conscious of his superiority as the climax of created things, to learn to know also his helplessness, as that too is one of the keys to the knowledge of God.

JALALUDDIN RUMI, THE MASNAVI

INTRODUCTION

Think of the human being as a guest house, suggests Jalaluddin Rumi in one of his most powerful works. Every morning something new arrives: a joy, a sadness, a meanness, or some other momentary awareness. Welcome them all. If there descends upon you a 'crowd of sorrows' that sweeps your house empty, treat all these 'guests' with respect—they may be clearing you out to make space for future joys and delights. Even your darkest thoughts and emotions—shame and malice—should be met with laughter and open arms. Each has been sent as a guide from beyond.

Jalaluddin Rumi, or simply 'Rumi' as he is more familiarly known in the West, was a Persian Sufi poet, scholar, theologian, and mystic of the thirteenth century. Born into a family of Islamic preachers originally from Balkh, in what is now Afghanistan, Rumi accompanied his parents as they migrated by caravan through several Muslim lands, before eventually settling in Konya in what is modern-day Turkey. It was here that he met Shams-i Tabrizi, a spiritual master and guide who, tradition holds, taught Rumi for a short time before mysteriously disappearing, said to have been killed by students resentful of their close relationship. Rumi's loss found expression in an outpouring of lyric poems written after Shams' death. After his own death a quarter of a century later, Rumi's disciples formed the Mewlewi Sufi order of 'Whirling Dervishes' who perform their remembrance of God through music and dance.

The great theme of Rumi's work is that of *tawhid*—union with the 'beloved', or the divine, and longing to restore that union. His message, as we have seen, is one of far-reaching acceptance. Whatever befalls us we are neither to resist nor even to grudgingly accept. Instead, we are to positively welcome each of the great variety of thoughts and emotions that sweep through us as meaningful aspects of life, each of which has their role to play. It is an approach to the problems of living that can be embraced by Muslim, Christian, Buddhist, and agnostic alike.

To approach the divine one must first break through the limitations associated with the human condition. The Sufi does this in part by cultivating the power of detachment in order to see reality as it is, rather than as our passions and prejudices would colour it: 'The satiated man and the hungry one do not see the same thing when they look at a loaf of bread.' The Sufi is also alert to the difficulties imposed by social convention: it has been said that the Sufi approach is to realize that man is, largely, 'a bundle of what are nowadays called conditionings—fixed ideas and prejudices, automatic responses sometimes which have occurred through the training of others'.[1] That can only be done through unorthodox methods—and, in particular, by calling upon fundamental elements which exist in every human that have not been suppressed or eliminated by the conditioning process.

The *Masnavi*, one of the best known and most influential works of Sufism, is a collection of stories and anecdotes incorporating a variety of Islamic wisdom but focused on this inward personal dimension so characteristic of Sufism. We have a story of a lion led astray by his own lack of faith in the munificence of the universe. We have a comparison of Chinese and Greek artists, the former who paint

1. Idries Shah, *The Sufis* (New York: Anchor Books, 1971), 134, 141.

and colour their house in the most elaborate way, whereas the latter simply cleanse their house of all filth and thereby allow the walls to reflect the multitudinous colours of the surroundings. And we have the story of the faqir who found the hidden treasure not 'out there' but nearer to him than his own neck-vein.

Among the most striking of the short fables is the tale of the elephant in the dark room. In that tale, it was too dark to see the elephant, so each of the visitors in the room explored it with their hands. Those who felt its trunk thought it was a water pipe; those who felt its ear thought it was a fan; and those who felt its leg thought it must be a pillar. In the darkness, none could obtain a complete picture; what may have been correct from a limited perspective may be totally incorrect from the larger perspective. Likewise, the Sufi seeker acknowledges he is temporarily out of contact with complete reality. But that only encourages him to cultivate new modes of perception and a broader, more inclusive view.

THE MASNAVI

THE LION AND THE BEASTS

In the book of Kalila and Damna a story is told of a lion who held all the beasts of the neighborhood in subjection, and was in the habit of making constant raids upon them, to take and kill such of them as he required for his daily food. At last the beasts took counsel together, and agreed to deliver up one of their company every day, to satisfy the lion's hunger, if he, on his part, would cease to annoy them by his continual forays. The lion was at first unwilling to trust to their promise, remarking that he always preferred to rely on his own exertions; but the beasts succeeded in persuading him that he would do well to trust Providence and their word. To illustrate the thesis that human exertions are vain, they related a story of a man who got Solomon to transport him to Hindustan to escape the angel of death, but was smitten by the angel the moment he got there. Having carried their point, the beasts continued for some time to perform their engagement. One day it came to the turn of the hare to be delivered up as a victim to the lion; but he requested the others to let him practice a stratagem. They scoffed at him, asking how such silly beast as he could pretend to outwit the lion. The hare assured them that wisdom was of God, and God might choose weak things to confound the strong. At last they consented to let him try his luck. He took his way slowly to the lion, and found him sorely enraged. In excuse for his tardy arrival he represented that he and another hare had set out together to appear before the lion, but a strange lion had seized the second hare, and carried it off in spite of his remonstrances. On hearing this, the lion was exceeding wroth, and commanded the hare to show him the foe who had trespassed on his preserves. Pretending to be afraid, the hare got the lion to take him upon his back, and directed him to a well. On looking down the well, the lion saw in the water the reflection of himself and of the hare on his back; and thinking that he saw his foe with the stolen hare, he plunged in to attack him, and was drowned, while the hare sprang off his back and escaped. This folly on the part of the lion was predestined to punish him for denying God's ruling providence. So Adam, though he knew the names of all things, in accordance with God's predestination, neglected to obey a single prohibition, and his disobedience cost him dearly.

Trust in God, as opposed to human exertions.

THE MERCHANT AND THE CLEVER PARROT

There was a certain merchant who kept a parrot in a cage. Being about to travel to Hindustan on business, he asked the parrot if he had any message to send to his kinsmen in that country, and the parrot desired him to tell them that he was kept confined in a cage. The merchant promised to deliver this message, and on reaching Hindustan, duly delivered it to the first flock of parrots he saw. On hearing it one of them at once fell down dead. The merchant was annoyed with his own parrot for having sent such a fatal message, and on his return home sharply rebuked his parrot for doing so. But the parrot no sooner heard the merchant's tale than he too fell down dead in his cage. The merchant, after lamenting his death, took his corpse out of the cage and threw it away; but, to his surprise, the corpse immediately recovered life, and flew away, explaining that the Hindustani parrot had only feigned death to suggest this way of escaping from confinement in a cage.

Saints are preserved from all harm.

THE LION WHO HUNTED WITH THE WOLF AND THE FOX

A lion took a wolf and a fox with him on a hunting excursion, and succeeded in catching a wild ox, an ibex, and a hare. He then directed the wolf to divide the prey. The wolf proposed to award the ox to the lion, the ibex to himself, and the hare to the fox. The lion was enraged with the wolf because he had presumed to talk of 'I' and 'you', and 'my share' and 'your share' when it all belonged of right to the lion, and he slew the wolf with one blow of his paw. Then, turning to the fox, he ordered him to make the division. The fox, rendered wary by the fate of the wolf, replied that the whole should be the portion of the lion. The lion, pleased with his self-abnegation, gave it all up to him, saying, 'Thou art no longer a fox, but myself'.

Till man destroys 'self' he is no true friend of God.

THE CHINESE AND THE GREEK ARTISTS

The Chinese and the Greeks disputed before the Sultan which of them were the better painters; and, in order to settle the dispute, the Sultan allotted to each a house to be painted by them. The Chinese procured all kinds of paints, and coloured their house in the most elaborate way. The Greeks, on the other hand, used no colours at all, but contented themselves with cleansing the walls of their house from all filth, and burnishing them till they were as clear and bright as the heavens. When the two houses were offered to the Sultan's inspection, that painted by the Chinese was much admired; but the Greek house carried off the palm, as all the colours of the other house were reflected on its walls with an endless variety of shades and hues.

THE ELEPHANT IN A DARK ROOM

Some Hindus were exhibiting an elephant in a dark room, and many people collected to see it. But as the place was too dark to permit them to see the elephant, they all felt it with their hands, to gain an idea of what it was like. One felt its trunk, and declared that the beast resembled a water-pipe; another felt its ear, and said it must be a large fan; another its leg, and thought it must be a pillar; another felt its back, and declared the beast must be like a great throne. According to the part which each felt, he gave a different description of the animal. One, as it were, called it 'Dal'[2] and another 'Alif'.[3]

THE LOVER WHO READS SONNETS TO HIS MISTRESS

A lover was once admitted to the presence of his mistress, but, instead of embracing her, he pulled out a paper of sonnets and read them to her, describing her perfections and charms and his own love towards her at length. His mistress said to him, 'You are now in my presence, and these lover's sighs and invocations are a waste of time. It is not the part of a true lover to waste his time in this way. It shows that I am not the real object of your affection, but that what you really love is your own effusions and ecstatic raptures. I see, as it were, the water which I have longed for before me, and yet you withhold it. I am, as it were, in Bulgaria, and the object of your love is in Cathay. One who is really loved is the single object of her lover, the Alpha and Omega of his desires. As for you, you are wrapped up in your own amorous raptures, depending on the varying states of your own feelings, instead of being wrapped up in me.'

The true mystic must not stop at mere subjective religious emotions, but seek absolute union with God.

2. A Sufi symbol for created things.
3. A Sufi symbol for God.

THE BOYS AND THEIR TEACHER

To illustrate the force of imagination or opinion, a story is told of a trick played by boys upon their master. The boys wished to obtain a holiday, and the sharpest of them suggested that when the master came into the school each boy should condole with him on his alleged sickly appearance. Accordingly, when he entered, one said, 'O master, how pale you are looking!' and another said, 'You are looking very ill today,' and so on. The master at first answered that there was nothing the matter with him, but as one boy after another continued assuring him that he looked very ill, he was at length deluded into imagining that he must really be ill. So he returned to his house, making the boys follow him there, and told his wife that he was not well, bidding her mark how pale he was. His wife assured him he was not looking pale, and offered to convince him by bringing a mirror; but he refused to look at it, and took to his bed. He then ordered the boys to begin their lessons; but they assured him that the noise made his head ache, and he believed them, and dismissed them to their homes, to the annoyance of their mothers.

THE SAGE AND THE PEACOCK

A sage went out to till his field, and saw a peacock busily engaged in destroying his own plumage with his beak. At seeing this insane self-destruction the sage could not refrain himself, but cried out to the peacock to forbear from mutilating himself and spoiling his beauty in so wanton a manner. The peacock then explained to him that the bright plumage which he admired so much was a fruitful source of danger to its unfortunate owner, as it led to his being constantly pursued by hunters, whom he had no strength to contend against; and he had accordingly decided on ridding himself of it with his own beak, and making himself so ugly that no hunter would in future care to molest him.

The poet proceeds to point out that worldly cleverness and accomplishments and wealth endanger man's spiritual life, like the peacock's plumage; but, nevertheless, they are appointed for our probation, and without such trials there can be no virtue.

THE FAQIR AND THE HIDDEN TREASURE

Notwithstanding the clear evidence of God's bounty, engendering these spiritual states in men, philosophers and learned men, wise in their own conceit, obstinately shut their eyes to it, and look afar off for what is really close to them, so that they incur the penalty of 'being branded on the nostrils', adjudged against unbelievers. This is illustrated by the story of a poor faqir[4] who prayed to God that he might be fed without being obliged to work for his

4. A Muslim mendicant.

food. A divine voice came to him in his sleep and directed him to go to the house of a certain scribe and take a certain writing that he should find there. He did so, and on reading the writing found that it contained directions for finding a hidden treasure. The directions were as follows: 'Go outside the city to the dome which covers the tomb of the martyr; turn your back to the tomb and your face towards Mecca, place an arrow in your bow, and where the arrow falls there dig for the treasure.' But before the faqir had time to commence the search the rumor of the writing and its contents had reached the king, who at once sent and took it away from the faqir, and began to search for the treasure on his own account. After shooting many arrows and digging in all directions the king failed to find the treasure, and got weary of searching, and returned the writing to the faqir. Then the faqir tried what he could do, but failed altogether to hit the spot where the treasure was buried. At last, despairing of success by his own unaided efforts, he cast his care upon God, and implored the divine assistance. Then a voice from heaven came to him, saying, 'You were directed to fix an arrow on your bow, but not to draw your bow with all your might, as you have been doing. Shoot as gently as possible, that the arrow may fall close to you, for the hidden treasure is indeed nearer to you than your neck-vein.'

Men overlook the spiritual treasures close to them.

BLAISE PASCAL, PENSÉES

INTRODUCTION

Imagine a number of men in chains, all condemned to death. Some are strangled every day in sight of others. Those who remain see their own predicament in the ones who have been eliminated. They are compelled, nevertheless, to wait their turn, looking at each other sorrowfully and without hope.

This, says Pascal, is the lot of man.

It may indeed be the case that we cannot say for certain whether God exists or does not. In the abstract, then, we might prefer to abstain from judgment. But we are 'engaged on the affair': since we are all thrown into the universe without our own choosing, and since we all will face death, we have no choice but to address ourselves to the central question.

Pascal's wager is probably the most ingenious of arguments for providing an answer. The wager itself goes like this. If you choose to believe in the existence of God, and you are proved right, then you will be rewarded with eternal life—infinite gain. If you choose to believe in God, and you are proved wrong, your loss will be finite and (relatively speaking) insignificant. Conversely, if you choose to disbelieve in God, and you are proved right, your gain for being right will be finite and (relatively speaking) insignificant. If you choose to disbelieve in God and you are proved wrong, however, your loss will be infinite.

The wager is rooted in game theory: if God exists, then it is infinitely more preferable to believe; if God does not exist, it doesn't make much difference whether you believe or not. Since we can't definitively establish God's existence or non-existence, it makes sense to believe.

Belief in God or, more loosely, a spiritual dimension, may be difficult to justify if we require strict proof. But many 'first principles' that we accept as true—space, time, motion, number—have not been independently proved; they are, in fact, the presuppositions upon which other proofs are built. In any event, in life we almost always operate on the basis of probability rather than certainty—the only certainties, as they say, being death and taxes. And as to God's nature, that must be totally incomprehensible to us, since by definition God has neither dimension nor limits.

Nobody—Pascal least of all—is asking for unthinking and unconditional belief in a supreme being. The world gives insufficient information to either prove or disprove the existence of God. Consider though, Pascal says, how many of our actions are based upon uncertainties. And in a state of uncertainty, the rational man does not blindly accept or reject: he instead assesses the benefits and risks of his belief. With so much to gain and so little to lose, the better choice, suggests Pascal, is obvious.

OF THE NEED OF SEEKING TRUTH.

SECOND PART. THAT MEN WITHOUT FAITH CANNOT KNOW THE TRUE GOOD, NOR JUSTICE.

All men seek happiness. To this there is no exception, what different means soever they employ, all tend to this goal. The reason that some men go to the wars and others avoid them is but the same desire attended in each with different views. Our will makes no steps but towards this object. This is the motive of every action of every man, even of him who hangs himself.

And yet after so many years, no one without faith has arrived at the point to which all eyes are turned.

All complain, princes and subjects, nobles and commons, old and young, strong and weak, learned and ignorant, sound and sick, of all countries, all times, all ages, and all conditions.

A trial so long, so constant and so uniform, should surely convince us of our inability to arrive at good by our own strength, but example teaches us but little. No resemblance is so exact but that there is some slight difference, and hence we expect that our endeavour will not be foiled on this occasion as before. Thus while the present never satisfies, experience deceives us, and from misfortune to misfortune leads us on to death, eternal crown of sorrows.

This desire, and this weakness cry aloud to us that there was once in man a true happiness, of which there now remains to him but the mark and the empty trace, which he vainly tries to fill from all that surrounds him, seeking from things absent the succour he finds not in things present; and these are all inadequate, because this infinite void can only be filled by an infinite and immutable object, that is to say, only by God himself.

He only is our true good, and since we have left him, it is strange that there is nothing in nature which has not served to take his place; neither the stars, nor heaven, earth, the elements, plants, cabbages, leeks, animals, insects, calves, serpents, fever, pestilence, war, famine, vices, adultery, incest. And since he has lost the true good, all things can equally appear good to him, even his own destruction, though so contrary to God, to reason, and to the whole course of nature.

Some seek good in authority, others in research and knowledge, others in pleasure. Others, who indeed are nearer the truth, have considered it necessary that the universal good which all men desire should not consist in any of those particular matters which can only be possessed by one, and which if once shared, afflict their possessor more by the want of what he has not, than they gladden him by the joy of what he has. They have apprehended that the true good should be such as all may possess at once, without diminution, and without envy, and that which none can lose against his will. And their reason is that this desire being natural to man, since it exists necessarily in all, and that all must have it, they conclude from it...

Infinite, nothing.—The soul of man is cast into the body, in which it finds number, time, dimension; it reasons thereon, and calls this nature or necessity, and cannot believe aught else.

Unity joined to infinity increases it not, any more than a foot measure added to infinite space. The finite is annihilated in presence of the infinite and becomes simply nought. Thus our intellect before God, thus our justice before the divine justice. There is not so great a disproportion between our justice and that of God, as between unity and infinity.

The justice of God must be as vast as his mercy,

but justice towards the reprobate is less vast, and should be less amazing than mercy towards the elect.

We know that there is an infinite, but are ignorant of its nature. As we know it to be false that numbers are finite, it must therefore be true that there is an infinity in number, but what this is we know not. It can neither be odd nor even, for the addition of a unit can make no change in the nature of number; yet it is a number, and every number is either odd or even, at least this is understood of every finite number.

Thus we may well know that there is a God, without knowing what he is.

We know then the existence and the nature of the finite, because we also are finite and have dimension.

We know the existence of the infinite, and are ignorant of its nature, because it has dimension like us, but not limits like us. But we know neither the existence nor the nature of God, because he has neither dimension nor limits.

But by faith we know his existence, by glory we shall know his nature. Now I have already shown that we can know well the existence of a thing without knowing its nature.

Let us now speak according to the light of nature.

If there be a God, he is infinitely incomprehensible, since having neither parts nor limits he has no relation to us. We are then incapable of knowing either what he is or if he is. This being so, who will dare to undertake the solution of the question? Not we, who have no relation to him.

Who then will blame Christians for not being able to give a reason for their faith; those who profess a religion for which they cannot give a reason? They declare in putting it forth to the world that it is a foolishness, *stultitiam,* and then you complain that they do not prove it. Were they to prove it they would not keep their word, it is in lacking proof that they are not lacking in sense.—Yes, but although this excuses those who offer it as such, and takes away from them the blame of putting it forth without reason, it does not excuse those who receive it.—Let us then examine this point, and say, 'God is, or he is not.' But to which side shall we incline? Reason can determine nothing about it. There is an infinite gulf fixed between us. A game is playing at the extremity of this infinite distance in which heads or tails may turn up. What will you wager? There is no reason for backing either one or the other, you cannot reasonably argue in favour of either.

Do not then accuse of error those who have already chosen, for you know nothing about it.—No, but I blame them for having made, not this choice, but a choice, for again both the man who calls 'heads' and his adversary are equally to blame, they are both in the wrong; the true course is not to wager at all.—

Yes, but you must wager; this depends not on your will, you are embarked in the affair. Which will you choose? Let us see. Since you must choose, let us see which least interests you. You have two things to lose, truth and good, and two things to stake, your reason and your will, your knowledge and your happiness; and your nature has two things to avoid, error and misery. Since you must needs choose, your reason is no more wounded in choosing one than the other. Here is one point cleared up, but what of your happiness? Let us weigh the gain and the loss in choosing heads that God is. Let us weigh the two cases: if you gain, you gain all; if you lose, you lose nothing. Wager then unhesitatingly that he is.—You are right. Yes, I must wager, but I may stake too much.—Let us see. Since there is an equal chance of gain and loss, if you had only to gain two lives for one, you might still wager. But were there three of them to gain, you would have to play, since needs must that you play, and you would be imprudent, since you must play, not to chance your life to gain three at a game where the chances of loss or gain are even. But there is an eternity of life and happiness. And that being so, were there an infinity of chances of which one only would be for you, you would still be right to stake one to win two, and you would act foolishly, being obliged to play, did you refuse to stake one life against three at a game in which out of an infinity of chances there be one for you, if there were an infinity of an infinitely happy life to win. But there is here an infinity of an infinitely happy life to win, a chance of gain against a finite number of chances of loss, and what you stake is finite; that is decided. Wherever the infinite exists and there is not an infinity of chances of loss against that of gain, there is no room for hesitation, you must risk the whole. Thus when a man is forced to play he must renounce reason to keep life, rather than hazard it for infinite gain, which is as likely to happen as the loss of nothingness.

For it is of no avail to say it is uncertain that we gain, and certain that we risk, and that the infinite distance between the certainty of that which is staked and the uncertainty of what we shall gain, equals the finite good which is certainly staked against an uncertain infinite. This is not so. Every gambler stakes a certainty to gain an uncertainty, and yet he stakes a finite certainty against a finite uncertainty without acting unreasonably. It is false to say there is infinite distance between the certain stake and the uncertain gain. There is in truth an infinity between the certainty of gain and the certainty of loss. But the uncertainty of gain is proportioned to the certainty of the stake, according to the proportion of chances of gain and loss, and if therefore there are as many chances on one side as on the other, the game is even. And thus the certainty of the venture is equal to the uncertainty of the winnings, so far is it from the truth that there is infinite distance between them. So that our argument is of infinite force, if we stake the finite in a game where there are equal chances of gain and loss, and the infinite is the winnings. This is demonstrable, and if men are capable of any truths, this is one.

I confess and admit it. Yet is there no means of

seeing the hands at the game?—Yes, the Scripture and the rest, etc.

—Well, but my hands are tied and my mouth is gagged: I am forced to wager and am not free, none can release me, but I am so made that I cannot believe. What then would you have me do?

True. But understand at least your incapacity to believe, since your reason leads you to belief and yet you cannot believe. Labour then to convince yourself, not by increase of the proofs of God, but by the diminution of your passions. You would fain arrive at faith, but know not the way; you would heal yourself of unbelief, and you ask remedies for it. Learn of those who have been bound as you are, but who now stake all that they possess; these are they who know the way you would follow, who are cured of a disease of which you would be cured. Follow the way by which they began, by making believe that they believed, taking the holy water, having masses said, etc. Thus you will naturally be brought to believe, and will lose your acuteness.—But that is just what I fear.—Why? what have you to lose?

But to show you that this is the right way, this it is that will lessen the passions, which are your great obstacles, etc.

What you say comforts and delights me, etc.—If my words please you, and seem to you cogent, know that they are those of one who has thrown himself on his knees before and after to pray that Being, infinite, and without parts, to whom he submits all his own being, that you also would submit to him all yours, for your own good and for his glory, and that this strength may be in accord with this weakness.

The end of this argument.—Now what evil will happen to you in taking this side? You will be trustworthy, honourable, humble, grateful, generous, friendly, sincere, and true. In truth you will no longer have those poisoned pleasures, glory and luxury, but you will have other pleasures. I tell you that you will gain in this life, at each step you make in this path you will see so much certainty of gain, so much nothingness in what you stake, that you will know at last that you have wagered on a certainty, an infinity, for which you have risked nothing.

Objection.—Those who hope for salvation are so far happy, but they have as a counterpoise the fear of hell.

Answer.—Who has most reason to fear hell, the man who is in ignorance if there be a hell, and who is certain of damnation if there be; or he who is certainly convinced that there is a hell, and has a hope of being saved if there be?

'I would soon have given up pleasure,' say they, 'had I but faith.' But I say to you, 'you would soon have faith did you leave off your pleasures. Now it is for you to begin. If I could, I would give you faith. I cannot do this, nor discover therefore if what you say is true. But you can easily give up pleasure, and discover if what I say is true.'

Probabilities.—We must live differently in the world, according to these different suppositions: 1. That we could always remain in it. 2. That it is certain we cannot remain here long, and uncertain if we shall remain here an hour. This last supposition is the case with us.

Instability.—It is horrible to feel all that we possess slipping away from us.

By the law of probabilities you are bound to take pains to seek the truth; for if you die without adoring the true source of all things you are lost. 'But,' say you, 'had he willed that I should adore him, he would have left me tokens of his will.' He has done so, but you neglect them. Seek them then, it is well worth your while.

Dungeon.—I admit that it is not necessary to fathom the opinion of Copernicus, but this: It is all our life is worth to know if the soul be mortal or immortal.

Fascinatio nugacitatis.—In order that passion may do no hurt, we should act as though we had but a week to live.

If we ought to give a week we ought to give our whole life.

In short, what is it you promise me if not ten years of self-love spent in trying hard to please without success, besides the troubles which are certain? For ten years is the probability.

Let us imagine a number of men in chains, all condemned to death, of whom some are strangled every day in the sight of the others, while those who remain see their own condition in that of their fellows, and wait their turn looking at each other sorrowfully and without hope. This is an image of the lot of man.

We must know ourselves, and if that does not serve to discover truth, it at least serves to regulate our lives, and there is nothing more just.

There are but three classes of persons: those who having found God, serve him; those who not having found him, diligently seek him; those who not having found him, live without seeking him. The first are happy and wise, the last are unhappy and fools, those between are unhappy, but they are wise.

It is certain that there is no good without the knowledge of God, that only as we approach him are we happy, and that the ultimate good is to know him certainly; that we are unhappy in proportion as we are removed from him, and that the greatest evil would be certainty of the opposite.

The ordinary world has the power of not thinking about what it does not choose to think about. 'Do not reflect on those passages about the Messiah,' said the Jew to his son. So our people often act. Thus false religions are preserved, and the true also, as regards many people.

But there are those who have not thus the power of preventing thought, and who think the more the more we forbid them. These get rid of false religions, and of the true also, if they do not find solid reasons.

If we ought to do nothing save on a certainty, we ought to do nothing for religion, for this is not certain. But how much we do on an uncertainty, as sea voyages, battles! I say then if this be the case we ought to do nothing at all, for nothing is certain, and that there is more certainty in religion than that we shall see another day, for it is not certain that we shall see tomorrow, but it is certainly possible that we shall not see it. We cannot say so much about religion. It is not certain that it is, but who will dare to say that it is certainly possible that it is not? But when we work for tomorrow, therefore for the uncertain, we act reasonably.

For we should work for the uncertain by the doctrine of chances already laid down.

We know truth, not only by the reason, but also by the heart, and it is from this last that we know first principles; and reason, which has nothing to do with it, tries in vain to combat them. The sceptics who desire truth alone labour in vain. We know that we do not dream, although it is impossible to prove it by reason, and this inability shows only the weakness of our reason, and not, as they declare, the general uncertainty of our knowledge. For our knowledge of first principles, as *space, time, motion, number,* is as distinct as any principle derived from reason. And reason must lean necessarily on this instinctive knowledge of the heart, and must found on it every process. We know instinctively that there are three dimensions in space, and that numbers are infinite, and reason then shows that there are no two square numbers one of which is double of the other. We feel principles, we infer propositions, both with certainty, though by different ways. It is as useless and absurd for reason to demand from the heart proofs of first principles before it will admit them, as it would be for the heart to ask from reason a feeling of all the propositions demonstrated before accepting them.

This inability should serve then only to humiliate reason, which would fain judge of all things, but not to shake our certainty, as if only reason were able to instruct us. Would to God, on the contrary, that we never needed reason, and that we knew everything by instinct and feeling! But nature has denied us this advantage, and has on the contrary given us but little knowledge of this kind, all the rest can be acquired by reason only.

Those to whom God has given religion by an instinctive feeling are very blessed, and quite convinced. But as for those who have it not, we can give it them only by reasoning, waiting for the time when God himself shall impress it on their heart, without which faith is useless for salvation.

Is then the soul too noble a subject for the feeble light of man? Let us then abase the soul to matter, and see if she knows whereof is made the very body which she animates, and those others which she contemplates and moves at her will. On this subject what have those great dogmatists known who are ignorant of nothing?

Harum sententiarum.[1]

This would no doubt suffice if reason were reasonable. She is reasonable enough to admit that she has never found anything stable, but she does not yet despair of reaching it; on the contrary, she is as ardent as ever in the search, and is sure that she has in herself all the necessary powers for this conquest.

We must therefore make an end, and after having examined these powers in their effects, recognise what they are in themselves, and see if reason has power and grasp capable of seizing the truth.

---

1. Harum sententiarum quo vera sit, Deus aliquis viderit: 'Of these opinions which is the true, let some god determine.' See Cicero, Tusculan Disputations, 1.23.

The preacher shows that man without God is wholly ignorant, and subject to inevitable misery. For to will and to be powerless is to be miserable. Now he wills to be happy, and to be assured of some truth, yet he can neither know, nor not desire to know. He cannot even doubt.

This is what I see and what troubles me. I look on all sides, and see nothing but obscurity, nature offers me nothing but matter for doubt and disquiet. Did I see nothing there which marked a Divinity I should decide not to believe in him. Did I see everywhere the marks of a Creator, I should rest peacefully in faith. But seeing too much to deny, and too little to affirm, my state is pitiful, and I have a hundred times wished that if God upheld nature, he would mark the fact unequivocally, but that if the signs which she gives of a God are fallacious, she would wholly suppress them, that she would either say all or say nothing, that I might see what part I should take. While in my present state, ignorant of what I am, and of what I ought to do, I know neither my condition nor my duty, my heart is wholly bent to know where is the true good in order to follow it, nothing would seem to me too costly for eternity.

ARTHUR SCHOPENHAUER, THE VANITY OF EXISTENCE

INTRODUCTION

Arthur Schopenhauer is one of the great proponents of what can be called 'atheist spirituality'.

Schopenhauer didn't believe in a personal God but his work displays a pronounced interest in the possibility of transcendence.

At the heart of existence, says Schopenhauer, is a 'Will' to live. Will is the 'lord of all worlds'—the driving force behind all phenomena—and everything belongs to it. It is restless and relentless. For humans, Will is comprised of two simple impulses—hunger and the sex drive—and is assisted at times by the effect of boredom. Every satisfaction of existing desire lays the seeds of some new desire, so that there is no end of it. It is blind and generally obtains very little recompense for all its incessant activity—its main achievement being just to keep the body together.

Life in general, then, is largely futile. But two aspects of this intrinsic futility stand out: life experienced in time; and life experienced as a task.

Time—considered deeply—poses a problem for us. We find ourselves suddenly existing after many thousands of years of non-existence, we exist for a short spell, and we are then (apparently) consigned back to non-existence. As if this wasn't disconcerting enough, we are condemned to live in an ever-passing present moment. That which *has been* (the past) exists no more; it exists as little as that which has *never* been (the future). While it may seem wise to embrace the present as the true reality, that too may be folly, since it cannot make sense to attach significance to something that passes away in an instant.

An equally difficult issue is posed by our pursuit of goals. We spend our whole life in striving after something or other we think will make us happy, and either we fail to obtain this goal, or we do obtain it only to be disappointed afterwards. Meanwhile, the present has been seen as something to put up with, serving only as a transition towards the goal. Many people at the end of life look back with regret to see that the very thing they let slip by unenjoyed was exactly the life in expectation of which they passed their time.

What, then, is the solution to this predicament?

The clue is in the 'opening of the way' that Schopenhauer associates with 'denial of the Will'. If the Will is that which traps us in this cycle of endless futility, overcoming the Will is the only way out. Denial of the Will opens the door to transcendence—to what Schopenhauer, in the otherwise relentlessly pessimistic 'Vanity of Existence', calls '*an infinite existence*, exposed to no attack from without, and needing nothing to support it'. It brings the possibility of a 'realm of eternal peace; some timeless, changeless state, one and undiversified'.

Schopenhauer didn't have space in 'The Vanity of Existence' to develop the theme, but he was able to do so his magnum opus, *The World as Will and Representation*.

There were, he thought, three principal ways to obtain liberation.

First, by means of aesthetic contemplation, we are able to transcend our default condition of remorseless desiring and willing. It is in the state of pure contemplation that we are delivered from the fierce pressure of the Will: we can raise ourselves above our desires and cares through a universal state of consciousness that is will-less, painless, and timeless.

161

Second, through moral awareness, we can begin to recognize each human as being one manifestation of the universal Will, and that the same humanity looks out from every one of us. As we share the same inner nature, so we all carry the same burden of humanity, and are able to come to terms with the human fallibility we encounter at every instant.

Finally, though, it is asceticism—denial of the Will—that brings the ultimate liberation. If the relentless hunger and craving of the Will is the source of man's suffering and degradation, it follows that the only route to full transcendence will come from renunciation, resignation, and Will-lessness. The ascetic—by denying the Will—is transformed into a 'pure knowing being' who becomes 'the undimmed mirror of the world'. It is the ascetic alone who obtains the gifts of calmness of spirit, deep tranquility, and unshakeable confidence and serenity.

Schopenhauer speaks directly to the modern condition. It is true that many of us, through choice or circumstance, are now subject to forces and pressures that have thrown our faith into question. But to live in a spiritual vacuum, as many are now finding, is enervating, dispiriting, and devoid of meaning. It doesn't need to be like that. It's possible to take a different approach. And—for the most sceptical among us in particular—we can begin here.

THE VANITY OF EXISTENCE

This vanity finds expression in the whole way in which things exist; in the infinite nature of Time and Space, as opposed to the finite nature of the individual in both; in the ever–passing present moment as the only mode of actual existence; in the interdependence and relativity of all things; in continual Becoming without ever Being; in constant wishing and never being satisfied; in the long battle which forms the history of life, where every effort is checked by difficulties, and stopped until they are overcome. Time is that in which all things pass away; it is merely the form under which the will to live—the thing–in–itself and therefore imperishable—has revealed to it that its efforts are in vain; it is that agent by which at every moment all things in our hands become as nothing, and lose any real value they possess.

That which *has been* exists no more; it exists as little as that which has *never* been. But of everything that exists you must say, in the next moment, that it has been. Hence something of great importance now past is inferior to something of little importance now present, in that the latter is a *reality*, and related to the former as something to nothing.

A man finds himself, to his great astonishment, suddenly existing, after thousands and thousands of years of non–existence: he lives for a little while; and then, again, comes an equally long period when he must exist no more. The heart rebels against this, and feels that it cannot be true. The crudest intellect cannot speculate on such a subject without having a presentiment that Time is something ideal in its nature. This ideality of Time and Space is the key to every true system of metaphysics; because it provides for quite another order of things than is to be met with in the domain of nature. This is why Kant is so great.

Of every event in our life we can say only for one moment that it *is*; forever after, that it *was*. Every evening we are poorer by a day. It might, perhaps, make us mad to see how rapidly our short span of time ebbs away; if it were not that in the furthest depths of our being we are secretly conscious of our share in the exhaustible spring of eternity, so that we can always hope to find life in it again.

Consideration of the kind, touched on above, might, indeed, lead us to embrace the belief that the greatest *wisdom* is to make the enjoyment of the present the supreme object of life; because that is the only reality, all else being merely the play of thought. On the other hand, such a course might just as well be called the greatest *folly*: for that which in the next moment exists no more, and vanishes utterly, like a dream, can never be worth a serious effort.

The whole foundation on which our existence rests is the present—the ever-fleeting present. It lies, then, in the very nature of our existence to take the form of constant motion, and to offer no possibility of our ever attaining the rest for which we are always striving. We are like a man running downhill, who cannot keep on his legs unless he runs on, and will inevitably fall if he stops; or, again, like a pole balanced on the tip of one's finger; or like a planet, which would fall into its sun the moment it ceased to hurry forward on its way. Unrest is the mark of existence.

In a world where all is unstable, and nought can endure, but is swept onwards at once in the hurrying whirlpool of change; where a man, if he is to keep erect at all, must always be advancing and moving, like an acrobat on a rope—in such a world, happiness in inconceivable. How can it dwell where, as Plato says, *continual Becoming and never Being* is the sole form of existence? In the first place, a man never is happy, but spends his whole life in striving after something which he thinks will make him so; he seldom attains his goal, and when he does, it is only to be disappointed; he is mostly shipwrecked in the end, and comes into harbor with masts and rigging gone. And then, it is all one whether he has been happy or miserable; for his life was never anything more than a present moment always vanishing; and now it is over.

At the same time it is a wonderful thing that, in the world of human beings as in that of animals in general, this manifold restless motion is produced and kept up by the agency of two simple impulses—hunger and the sexual instinct; aided a little, perhaps, by the influence of boredom, but by

165

nothing else; and that, in the theatre of life, these suffice to form the *primum mobile*[1] of how complicated a machinery, setting in motion how strange and varied a scene!

On looking a little closer, we find that inorganic matter presents a constant conflict between chemical forces, which eventually works dissolution; and on the other hand, that organic life is impossible without continual change of matter, and cannot exist if it does not receive perpetual help from without. This is the realm of finality; and its opposite would be *an infinite existence*, exposed to no attack from without, and needing nothing to support it; the realm of eternal peace; some timeless, changeless state, one and undiversified; the negative knowledge of which forms the dominant note of the Platonic philosophy. It is to some such state as this that the denial of the will to live opens up the way.

The scenes of our life are like pictures done in rough mosaic. Looked at close, they produce no effect. There is nothing beautiful to be found in them, unless you stand some distance off. So, to gain anything we have longed for is only to discover how vain and empty it is; and even though we are always living in expectation of better things, at the same time we often repent and long to have the past back again. We look upon the present as something to be put up with while it lasts, and serving only as the way

1. First mover.

towards our goal. Hence most people, if they glance back when they come to the end of life, will find that all along they have been living *ad interim*:[2] they will be surprised to find that the very thing they disregarded and let slip by unenjoyed, was just the life in the expectation of which they passed all their time. Of how many a man may it not be said that hope made a fool of him until he danced into the arms of death!

Then again, how insatiable a creature is man! Every satisfaction he attains lays the seeds of some new desire, so that there is no end to the wishes of each individual will. And why is this? The real reason is simply that, taken in itself, Will is the lord of all worlds: everything belongs to it, and therefore no one single thing can ever give it satisfaction, but only the whole, which is endless. For all that, it must rouse our sympathy to think how very little the Will, this lord of the world, really gets when it takes the form of an individual; usually only just enough to keep the body together. This is why man is so very miserable.

Life presents itself chiefly as a task—the task, I mean, of subsisting at all, *gagner sa vie*.[3] If this is accomplished, life is a burden, and then there comes the second task of doing something with that which has been won—of warding off boredom, which, like a bird of prey, hovers over us, ready to fall wherever it sees a life secure from need. The first task is to win

---

2. For the intervening time.
3. To make a living.

something; the second, to banish the feeling that it has been won; otherwise it is a burden.

Human life must be some kind of mistake. The truth of this will be sufficiently obvious if we only remember that man is a compound of needs and necessities hard to satisfy; and that even when they are satisfied, all he obtains is a state of painlessness, where nothing remains to him but abandonment to boredom. This is direct proof that existence has no real value in itself; for what is boredom but the feeling of the emptiness of life? If life—the craving for which is the very essence of our being—were possessed of any positive intrinsic value, there would be no such thing as boredom at all: mere existence would satisfy us in itself, and we should want for nothing. But as it is, we take no delight in existence except when we are struggling for something; and then distance and difficulties to be overcome make our goal look as though it would satisfy us—an illusion which vanishes when we reach it; or else when we are occupied with some purely intellectual interest—when in reality we have stepped forth from life to look upon it from the outside, much after the manner of spectators at a play. And even sensual pleasure itself means nothing but a struggle and aspiration, ceasing the moment its aim is attained. Whenever we are not occupied in one of these ways, but cast upon existence itself, its vain and worthless nature is brought home to us; and this is what we mean by boredom. The hankering after what is strange and uncommon—an innate and ineradicable tendency of human nature—shows how glad we are at any interruption of that natural course of affairs which is so very tedious.

That this most perfect manifestation of the will to live, the human organism, with the cunning and complex working of its machinery, must fall to dust and yield up itself and all its strivings to extinction—this is the naive way in which Nature, who is always so true and sincere in what she says, proclaims the whole struggle of this will as in its very essence barren and unprofitable. Were it of any value in itself, anything unconditioned and absolute, it could not thus end in mere nothing.

If we turn from contemplating the world as a whole, and, in particular, the generations of men as they live their little hour of mock–existence and then are swept away in rapid succession; if we turn from this, and look at life in its small details, as presented, say, in a comedy, how ridiculous it all seems! It is like a drop of water seen through a microscope, a single drop teeming with *infusoria*;[4] or a speck of cheese full of mites invisible to the naked eye. How we laugh as they bustle about so eagerly, and struggle with one another in so tiny a space! And whether here, or in the little span of human life, this terrible activity produces a comic effect.

4. Minute organisms found especially in water with decomposing organic matter.

It is only in the microscope that our life looks so big. It is an indivisible point, drawn out and magnified by the powerful lenses of Time and Space.

13

FRIEDRICH NIETZSCHE, THUS SPOKE ZARATHUSTRA

INTRODUCTION

Spirituality contains within it the urge for transcendence.

In sceptical and atheistic times, however, what possibility will there be for that?

One of the best answers to that question is given by Friedrich Nietzsche in *Thus Spoke Zarathustra*. This is the work that famously pronounced that 'God is dead'. But Nietzsche's genius is not to leave it there. Instead, he reconfigures transcendence for a godless age as a kind of 'self-overcoming' more pressing and urgent than ever before.

The book tells of the fictitious travels and speeches of Zarathustra. Zarathustra (more commonly known in English as Zoroaster) was a prophet and founder of the ancient Persian faith of Zoroastrianism. In Zoroastrian belief, the universe is the site of a 3,000-year struggle between good and evil, which will be punctuated by evil's final assault, and concluded by the final triumph of good over evil. It has been said that Zoroaster is responsible for introducing 'good' and 'evil' as the basic competing forces in the universe and has been considered the originator of traditional morality.

It is a totally new and different Zarathustra, however, who speaks to us in *Thus Spoke Zarathustra*.

We first meet Zarathustra on the mountain where he has resided in solitude for ten years. He is weary of accumulating wisdom where there is no one to share it with, so he decides to go down to the towns and cities below. In a forest on the way down he meets an old hermit who has turned away from the world of men and devoted himself to God. Zarathustra's reaction is the first indication that the spiritual perspective he brings will be quite unlike anything that has come before—for it is here that he makes the historic proclamation that 'God is dead'.

Zarathustra arrives next at the marketplace of the nearest town. He now begins to teach his revolutionary doctrine of the 'self-overcoming' of man: man is compared to a ropedancer who must cross over from his current existence as a two-legged animal to realize his full potentiality as 'Superman'. At the same time he warns of the consequences of rejecting this teaching—namely, the inevitable decline of humanity towards existence as degraded 'last men', festering in their own mediocrity. It transpires that there is, in fact, a literal ropedancer in the town. The ropedancer begins his performance upon a rope stretched between two towers, but is surprised by a little buffoon who jumps out from behind him, leaps over him, and causes him to fall to the ground with fatal consequences. Zarathustra understands the meaning of what he has seen: the old, servile, degraded ways of mankind, represented by the buffoon, remain strong enough to impede the transition towards the 'Superman'. Zarathustra leaves the town. The great mass of men is not yet ready for his teaching. He must seek not herds to follow him but companions and co-creators who will understand and appreciate his mission.

Of this teaching, it is the doctrine of the 'Superman' or *Übermensch* that is both the most important and the most controversial. The essence of the doctrine is that man, in his current state, is something to be surpassed. There are several aspects of this 'overcoming'. There is the overcoming of traditional religion and morality, which are no longer fit for purpose. There is the overcoming of nihilism, which threatens to overwhelm the lesser man with hopelessness. And there is overcoming of self and the weaknesses and limitations associated with it.

Zarathustra contrasts his Superman with another kind of man he calls 'the last man'. The 'last man' is the equal of all other men and shares the same desires with them. He loves his neighbour and has discovered happiness. But he is a herd creature—fit neither to rule nor obey. He makes everything small. And true depth of experience escapes him: 'What is love? What is creation? What is longing? What is a star?'—these are questions in response to which the 'last man' can only blink in total incomprehension.

Self-overcoming is one aspect of the 'will to power'—the organizing principle or 'life-will' of the universe. Will to power, says Nietzsche, is everywhere. It is equally present in the dictates of traditional morality (which express the will to power of its proponents) as it is in the will of the servant (who would be master over a 'still weaker one'). Even in the fall and perishing of a leaf there is the will to power of life sacrificing itself in favour of future growth. The superior man through his own self-overcoming aligns himself with this universal law.

Thus Spoke Zarathustra is a remarkable work that makes for an uncomfortable read. It points to a form of transcendence that is premised upon releasing the hitherto unrecognized potentials of our nature—but it does so by urging us to look upon ourselves with contempt as transitional beings falling somewhere between monkey and god.

It is, of course, reasonably clear from where we stand, at the beginning of the twenty-first century, that contemporary society has rejected the *Übermensch*. Like Nietzsche's 'last men', we have turned away from the heroic individual and seek safety in the herd. We take pride in our equalism and view sameness as a virtue. We have embraced our littleness and finally put the doctrine of 'self-overcoming' to rest.

Or have we?

ZARATHUSTRA'S PROLOGUE

1. When Zarathustra was thirty years old, he left his home and the lake of his home, and went into the mountains. There he enjoyed his spirit and his solitude, and for ten years did not weary of it. But at last his heart changed, and rising one morning with the rosy dawn, he went before the sun, and spoke thus unto it:

You great star! What would be your happiness if you had not those for whom you shine!

For ten years have you climbed hither unto my cave: you would have wearied of your light and of the journey, had it not been for me, my eagle, and my serpent.

But we awaited you every morning, took from you your overflow, and blessed you for it.

175

Lo! I am weary of my wisdom, like the bee that has gathered too much honey; I need hands outstretched to take it.

I would fain bestow and distribute, until the wise have once more become joyous in their folly, and the poor happy in their riches.

Therefore must I descend into the deep: as you do in the evening, when you go behind the sea, and give light also to the nether-world, you exuberant star!

Like you must I *go down*, as men say, to whom I shall descend.

Bless me, then, you tranquil eye, that can behold even the greatest happiness without envy!

Bless the cup that is about to overflow, that the water may flow golden out of it, and carry everywhere the reflection of your bliss!

Lo! This cup is again going to empty itself, and Zarathustra is again going to be a man.

Thus began Zarathustra's down-going.

2. Zarathustra went down the mountain alone, no one meeting him. When he entered the forest, however, there suddenly stood before him an old man, who had left his holy cot to seek roots. And thus spoke the old man to Zarathustra:

'No stranger to me is this wanderer: many years ago passed he by. Zarathustra he was called; but he has altered.

Then you carried your ashes into the mountains:

will you now carry your fire into the valleys? Do you fear the incendiary's doom?

Yea, I recognise Zarathustra. Pure is his eye, and no loathing lurks about his mouth. Goes he not along like a dancer?

Altered is Zarathustra; a child has Zarathustra become; an awakened one is Zarathustra: what will you do in the land of the sleepers?

As in the sea have you lived in solitude, and it has borne you up. Alas, will you now go ashore? Alas, will you again drag your body yourself?'

Zarathustra answered: 'I love mankind.'

'Why,' said the saint, 'did I go into the forest and the desert? Was it not because I loved men far too well?

Now I love God: men, I do not love. Man is a thing too imperfect for me. Love to man would be fatal to me.'

Zarathustra answered: 'What spoke I of love! I am bringing gifts unto men.'

'Give them nothing,' said the saint. 'Take rather part of their load, and carry it along with them—that will be most agreeable unto them: if only it be agreeable unto you!

If, however, you will give unto them, give them no more than an alms, and let them also beg for it!'

'No,' replied Zarathustra, 'I give no alms. I am not poor enough for that.'

The saint laughed at Zarathustra, and spoke thus: 'Then see to it that they accept your treasures! They are distrustful of anchorites, and do not believe that we come with gifts.

The fall of our footsteps rings too hollow through their streets. And just as at night, when they are in bed and hear a man abroad long before sunrise, so they ask themselves concerning us: Where goes the thief?

Go not to men, but stay in the forest! Go rather to the animals! Why not be like me—a bear amongst bears, a bird amongst birds?'

'And what does the saint in the forest?' asked Zarathustra.

The saint answered: 'I make hymns and sing them; and in making hymns I laugh and weep and mumble: thus do I praise God.

With singing, weeping, laughing, and mumbling do I praise the God who is my God. But what do you bring us as a gift?'

When Zarathustra had heard these words, he bowed to the saint and said: 'What should I have to give you! Let me rather hurry hence lest I take aught away from you!'—And thus they parted from one another, the old man and Zarathustra, laughing like schoolboys.

When Zarathustra was alone, however, he said to his heart: 'Could it be possible! This old saint in the forest hath not yet heard of it, that *God is dead!*'

3. When Zarathustra arrived at the nearest town which adjoined the forest, he found many people

assembled in the marketplace; for it had been announced that a ropedancer would give a performance. And Zarathustra spoke thus unto the people:

I teach you the Superman. Man is something that is to be surpassed. What have you done to surpass man?

All beings hitherto have created something beyond themselves: and you want to be the ebb of that great tide, and would rather go back to the beast than surpass man?

What is the ape to man? A laughing-stock, a thing of shame. And just the same shall man be to the Superman: a laughing-stock, a thing of shame.

You have made your way from the worm to man, and much within you is still worm. Once were you apes, and even yet man is more of an ape than any of the apes.

Even the wisest among you is only a disharmony and hybrid of plant and phantom. But do I bid you become phantoms or plants?

Lo, I teach you the Superman!

The Superman is the meaning of the earth. Let your will say: The Superman *shall be* the meaning of the earth!

I conjure you, my brethren, *remain true to the earth*, and believe not those who speak unto you of superearthly hopes! Poisoners are they, whether they know it or not.

Despisers of life are they, decaying ones and

poisoned ones themselves, of whom the earth is weary: so away with them!

Once blasphemy against God was the greatest blasphemy; but God died, and therewith also those blasphemers. To blaspheme the earth is now the dreadfulest sin, and to rate the heart of the unknowable higher than the meaning of the earth!

Once the soul looked contemptuously on the body, and then that contempt was the supreme thing—the soul wished the body meagre, ghastly, and famished. Thus it thought to escape from the body and the earth.

Oh, that soul was itself meagre, ghastly, and famished; and cruelty was the delight of that soul!

But you, also, my brethren, tell me: What doth your body say about your soul? Is your soul not poverty and pollution and wretched self-complacency?

Verily, a polluted stream is man. One must be a sea, to receive a polluted stream without becoming impure.

Lo, I teach you the Superman: he is that sea; in him can your great contempt be submerged.

What is the greatest thing you can experience? It is the hour of great contempt. The hour in which even your happiness becomes loathsome unto you, and so also your reason and virtue.

The hour when you say: 'What good is my happiness! It is poverty and pollution and wretched self-complacency. But my happiness should justify existence itself!'

The hour when you say: 'What good is my reason! Does it long for knowledge as the lion for his food? It is poverty and pollution and wretched self-complacency!'

The hour when you say: 'What good is my virtue! As yet it has not made me passionate. How weary I am of my good and my bad! It is all poverty and pollution and wretched self-complacency!'

The hour when you say: 'What good is my justice! I do not see that I am fervour and fuel. The just, however, are fervour and fuel!'

The hour when we say: 'What good is my pity! Is not pity the cross on which he is nailed who loves man? But my pity is not a crucifixion.'

Have you ever spoken thus? Have you ever cried thus? Ah! would that I had heard you crying thus!

It is not your sin—it is your self-satisfaction that cries unto heaven; your very sparingness in sin cries unto heaven!

Where is the lightning to lick you with its tongue? Where is the frenzy with which you should be inoculated?

Lo, I teach you the Superman: he is that lightning, he is that frenzy!

When Zarathustra had thus spoken, one of the people called out: 'We have now heard enough of the ropedancer; it is time now for us to see him!' And all the people laughed at Zarathustra. But the ropedancer, who thought the words applied to him, began his performance.

4. Zarathustra, however, looked at the people and wondered. Then he spoke thus:

Man is a rope stretched between the animal and the Superman—a rope over an abyss.

A dangerous crossing, a dangerous wayfaring, a dangerous looking-back, a dangerous trembling and halting.

What is great in man is that he is a bridge and not a goal: what is lovable in man is that he is an *over-going* and a *down-going*.

I love those that know not how to live except as down-goers, for they are the over-goers.

I love the great despisers, because they are the great adorers, and arrows of longing for the other shore.

I love those who do not first seek a reason beyond the stars for going down and being sacrifices, but sacrifice themselves to the earth, that the earth of the Superman may hereafter arrive.

I love him who lives in order to know, and seeks to know in order that the Superman may hereafter live. Thus seeks he his own down-going.

I love him who labours and invents, that he may build the house for the Superman, and prepare for him earth, animal, and plant: for thus seeks he his own down-going.

I love him who loves his virtue: for virtue is the will to down-going, and an arrow of longing.

I love him who reserves no share of spirit for

himself, but wants to be wholly the spirit of his virtue: thus walks he as spirit over the bridge.

I love him who makes his virtue his inclination and destiny: thus, for the sake of his virtue, he is willing to live on, or live no more.

I love him who desires not too many virtues. One virtue is more of a virtue than two, because it is more of a knot for one's destiny to cling to.

I love him whose soul is lavish, who wants no thanks and does not give back: for he always bestows, and desires not to keep for himself.

I love him who is ashamed when the dice fall in his favour, and who then asks: 'Am I a dishonest player?'—for he is willing to succumb.

I love him who scatters golden words in advance of his deeds, and always does more than he promises: for he seeks his own down-going.

I love him who justifies the future ones, and redeems the past ones: for he is willing to succumb through the present ones.

I love him who chastens his God, because he loves his God: for he must succumb through the wrath of his God.

I love him whose soul is deep even in the wounding, and may succumb through a small matter: thus goes he willingly over the bridge.

I love him whose soul is so overfull that he forgets himself, and all things are in him: thus all things become his down-going.

I love him who is of a free spirit and a free heart:

thus is his head only the bowels of his heart; his heart, however, causes his down-going.

I love all who are like heavy drops falling one by one out of the dark cloud that lowers over man: they herald the coming of the lightning, and succumb as heralds.

Lo, I am a herald of the lightning, and a heavy drop out of the cloud: the lightning, however, is the *Superman*.

5. When Zarathustra had spoken these words, he again looked at the people, and was silent. 'There they stand,' said he to his heart; 'there they laugh: they understand me not; I am not the mouth for these ears.

Must one first batter their ears, that they may learn to hear with their eyes? Must one clatter like kettledrums and penitential preachers? Or do they only believe the stammerer?

They have something whereof they are proud. What do they call it, that which makes them proud? Culture, they call it; it distinguishes them from the goatherds.

They dislike, therefore, to hear of 'contempt' of themselves. So I will appeal to their pride.

I will speak unto them of the most contemptible thing: that, however, is *the last man!*'

And thus spoke Zarathustra unto the people:

It is time for man to fix his goal. It is time for man to plant the germ of his highest hope.

Still is his soil rich enough for it. But that soil will

one day be poor and exhausted, and no lofty tree will any longer be able to grow thereon.

Alas! there comes the time when man will no longer launch the arrow of his longing beyond man—and the string of his bow will have unlearned to whizz!

I tell you: one must still have chaos in one, to give birth to a dancing star. I tell you: you have still chaos in you.

Alas! There comes the time when man will no longer give birth to any star. Alas! There comes the time of the most despicable man, who can no longer despise himself.

Lo! I show you *the last man*.

'What is love? What is creation? What is longing? What is a star?'—so asks the last man and blinks.

The earth has then become small, and on it there hops the last man who makes everything small. His species is ineradicable like that of the ground-flea; the last man lives longest.

'We have discovered happiness'—say the last men, and blink thereby.

They have left the regions where it is hard to live; for they need warmth. One still loves one's neighbour and rubs against him; for one needs warmth.

Turning ill and being distrustful, they consider sinful: they walk warily. He is a fool who still stumbles over stones or men!

A little poison now and then: that makes pleasant dreams. And much poison at last for a pleasant death.

One still works, for work is a pastime. But one is careful lest the pastime should hurt one.

One no longer becomes poor or rich; both are too burdensome. Who still wants to rule? Who still wants to obey? Both are too burdensome.

No shepherd, and one herd! Everyone wants the same; everyone is equal: he who hath other sentiments goes voluntarily into the madhouse.

'Formerly all the world was insane,' say the subtlest of them, and blink thereby.

They are clever and know all that has happened: so there is no end to their raillery. People still fall out, but are soon reconciled—otherwise it spoils their stomachs.

They have their little pleasures for the day, and their little pleasures for the night, but they have a regard for health.

'We have discovered happiness,' say the last men, and blink thereby.

And here ended the first discourse of Zarathustra, which is also called 'The Prologue': for at this point the shouting and mirth of the multitude interrupted him. 'Give us this last man, O Zarathustra,' they called out 'make us into these last men! Then will we make you a present of the Superman!' And all the people exulted and smacked their lips. Zarathustra, however, turned sad, and said to his heart:

'They understand me not: I am not the mouth for these ears.

Too long, perhaps, have I lived in the mountains;

too much have I hearkened unto the brooks and trees: now do I speak unto them as unto the goatherds.

Calm is my soul, and clear, like the mountains in the morning. But they think me cold, and a mocker with terrible jests.

And now do they look at me and laugh: and while they laugh they hate me too. There is ice in their laughter.'

6. Then, however, something happened which made every mouth mute and every eye fixed. In the meantime, of course, the ropedancer had commenced his performance: he had come out at a little door, and was going along the rope which was stretched between two towers, so that it hung above the marketplace and the people. When he was just midway across, the little door opened once more, and a gaudily-dressed fellow like a buffoon sprang out, and went rapidly after the first one. 'Go on, halt-foot,' cried his frightful voice, 'go on, lazy-bones, interloper, sallow-face!—lest I tickle you with my heel! What do you here between the towers? In the tower is the place for you, you should be locked up; to one better than yourself you block the way!' And with every word he came nearer and nearer the first one. When, however, he was but a step behind, there happened the frightful thing which made every mouth mute and every eye fixed—he uttered a yell like a devil, and jumped over the other who was in his way. The latter, however, when he thus saw his rival triumph, lost at

the same time his head and his footing on the rope; he threw his pole away, and shot downwards faster than it, like an eddy of arms and legs, into the depth. The marketplace and the people were like the sea when the storm comes on: they all flew apart and in disorder, especially where the body was about to fall.

Zarathustra, however, remained standing, and just beside him fell the body, badly injured and disfigured, but not yet dead. After a while consciousness returned to the shattered man, and he saw Zarathustra kneeling beside him. 'What are you doing there?' said he at last, 'I knew long ago that the devil would trip me up. Now he drags me to hell: will you prevent him?'

'On my honour, my friend,' answered Zarathustra, 'there is nothing of all that whereof you speak: there is no devil and no hell. Your soul will be dead even sooner than your body: fear, therefore, nothing anymore!'

The man looked up distrustfully.

'If you speak the truth,' said he, 'I lose nothing when I lose my life. I am not much more than an animal which has been taught to dance by blows and scanty fare.'

'Not at all,' said Zarathustra, 'you have made danger your calling; therein there is nothing contemptible. Now you perish by your calling: therefore will I bury you with my own hands.'

When Zarathustra had said this the dying one did

not reply further; but he moved his hand as if he sought the hand of Zarathustra in gratitude.

7. Meanwhile the evening came on, and the marketplace veiled itself in gloom. Then the people dispersed, for even curiosity and terror become fatigued. Zarathustra, however, still sat beside the dead man on the ground, absorbed in thought: so he forgot the time. But at last it became night, and a cold wind blew upon the lonely one. Then arose Zarathustra and said to his heart:

Verily, a fine catch of fish has Zarathustra made today! It is not a man he has caught, but a corpse.

Sombre is human life, and as yet without meaning: a buffoon may be fateful to it.

I want to teach men the sense of their existence, which is the Superman, the lightning out of the dark cloud—man.

But still am I far from them, and my sense speaks not unto their sense. To men I am still something between a fool and a corpse.

Gloomy is the night, gloomy are the ways of Zarathustra. Come, you cold and stiff companion! I carry you to the place where I shall bury you with mine own hands.

8. When Zarathustra had said this to his heart, he put the corpse upon his shoulders and set out on his way. Yet had he not gone a hundred steps, when there stole a man up to him and whispered in his ear—and

lo! he that spoke was the buffoon from the tower. 'Leave this town, O Zarathustra,' said he, 'there are too many here who hate you. The good and just hate you, and call you their enemy and despiser; the believers in the orthodox belief hate you, and call you a danger to the multitude. It was your good fortune to be laughed at: and verily you spoke like a buffoon. It was your good fortune to associate with the dead dog; by so humiliating yourself you have saved your life today. Depart, however, from this town—or tomorrow I shall jump over you, a living man over a dead one.' And when he had said this, the buffoon vanished; Zarathustra, however, went on through the dark streets.

At the gate of the town the gravediggers met him: they shone their torch on his face, and, recognising Zarathustra, they sorely derided him. 'Zarathustra is carrying away the dead dog: a fine thing that Zarathustra hath turned a gravedigger! For our hands are too cleanly for that roast. Will Zarathustra steal the bite from the devil? Well then, good luck to the repast! If only the devil is not a better thief than Zarathustra!—he will steal them both, he will eat them both!' And they laughed among themselves, and put their heads together.

Zarathustra made no answer thereto, but went on his way. When he had gone on for two hours, past forests and swamps, he had heard too much of the hungry howling of the wolves, and he himself became hungry. So he halted at a lonely house in which a light was burning.

'Hunger attacks me,' said Zarathustra, 'like a robber. Among forests and swamps my hunger attacks me, and late in the night.

'Strange humours has my hunger. Often it comes to me only after a repast, and all day it has failed to come: where has it been?'

And thereupon Zarathustra knocked at the door of the house. An old man appeared, who carried a light, and asked: 'Who comes unto me and my bad sleep?'

'A living man and a dead one,' said Zarathustra. 'Give me something to eat and drink, I forgot it during the day. He that feeds the hungry refreshes his own soul, says wisdom.'

The old man withdrew, but came back immediately and offered Zarathustra bread and wine. 'A bad country for the hungry,' said he; 'that is why I live here. Animal and man come unto me, the anchorite. But bid your companion eat and drink also, he is wearier than you.' Zarathustra answered: 'My companion is dead; I shall hardly be able to persuade him to eat.' 'That does not concern me,' said the old man sullenly; 'he that knocks at my door must take what I offer him. Eat, and fare you well!'

Thereafter Zarathustra again went on for two hours, trusting to the path and the light of the stars: for he was an experienced night-walker, and liked to look into the face of all that slept. When the morning dawned, however, Zarathustra found himself in a thick forest, and no path was any longer visible. He then put the dead man in a hollow tree at his head—for he wanted to protect him from the wolves—and laid himself down on the ground and moss. And immediately he fell asleep, tired in body, but with a tranquil soul.

9. Long slept Zarathustra; and not only the rosy dawn passed over his head, but also the morning. At last, however, his eyes opened, and amazedly he gazed into the forest and the stillness, amazedly he gazed into himself. Then he arose quickly, like a seafarer who all at once sees the land; and he shouted for joy: for he saw a new truth. And he spoke thus to his heart:

A light has dawned upon me: I need companions—living ones; not dead companions and corpses, which I carry with me where I will.

But I need living companions, who will follow me because they want to follow themselves—and to the place where I will. A light has dawned upon me. Not to the people is Zarathustra to speak, but to companions! Zarathustra shall not be the herd's herdsman and hound!

To allure many from the herd—for that purpose have I come. The people and the herd must be angry with me: a robber shall Zarathustra be called by the herdsmen.

Herdsmen, I say, but they call themselves the good

and just. Herdsmen, I say, but they call themselves the believers in the orthodox belief.

Behold the good and just! Whom do they hate most? Him who breaks up their tables of values, the breaker, the lawbreaker—he, however, is the creator.

Behold the believers of all beliefs! Whom do they hate most? Him who breaks up their tables of values, the breaker, the law-breaker—he, however, is the creator.

Companions, the creator seeks, not corpses—and not herds or believers either. Fellow-creators the creator seeks—those who grave new values on new tables.

Companions, the creator seeks, and fellow-reapers: for everything is ripe for the harvest with him. But he lacks the hundred sickles: so he plucks the ears of corn and is vexed.

Companions, the creator seeks, and such as know how to whet their sickles. Destroyers, will they be called, and despisers of good and evil. But they are the reapers and rejoicers.

Fellow-creators, Zarathustra seeks; fellow-reapers and fellow-rejoicers, Zarathustra seeks: what has he to do with herds and herdsmen and corpses!

And you, my first companion, rest in peace! Well have I buried you in your hollow tree; well have I hid you from the wolves.

But I part from you; the time has arrived. 'Twixt rosy dawn and rosy dawn there came unto me a new truth.

I am not to be a herdsman, I am not to be a grave-digger. Not anymore will I discourse unto the people; for the last time have I spoken unto the dead.

With the creators, the reapers, and the rejoicers will I associate: the rainbow will I show them, and all the stairs to the Superman.

To the lone-dwellers will I sing my song, and to the twain-dwellers; and unto him who has still ears for the unheard, will I make the heart heavy with my happiness.

I make for my goal, I follow my course; over the loitering and tardy will I leap. Thus let my on-going be their down-going!

10. This had Zarathustra said to his heart when the sun stood at noon-tide. Then he looked inquiringly aloft, for he heard above him the sharp call of a bird. And behold! An eagle swept through the air in wide circles, and on it hung a serpent, not like a prey, but like a friend: for it kept itself coiled round the eagle's neck.

'They are my animals,' said Zarathustra, and rejoiced in his heart.

'The proudest animal under the sun, and the wisest animal under the sun— they have come out to reconnoitre.

They want to know whether Zarathustra still lives. Verily, do I still live?

More dangerous have I found it among men than

among animals; in dangerous paths goes Zarathustra. Let my animals lead me!

When Zarathustra had said this, he remembered the words of the saint in the forest. Then he sighed and spoke thus to his heart:

'Would that I were wiser! Would that I were wise from the very heart, like my serpent!

But I am asking the impossible. Therefore do I ask my pride to go always with my wisdom!

And if my wisdom should some day forsake me—alas! it loves to fly away!—may my pride then fly with my folly!'

Thus began Zarathustra's down-going.

14

JAMES ALLEN, AS A MAN THINKETH

INTRODUCTION

One of the core beliefs of several spiritual traditions is that—to a greater or lesser extent and whether actually or metaphorically—'all is mind'. We've seen this principle in the inner spiritual tradition of Western Hermeticism as represented in *The Kybalion*. We've seen it in the Buddhist teachings contained in the *Dhammapada*: 'All that we are,' says the Buddha, 'is a result of what we have thought.' We've seen it in the Taoist doctrine that the 'Tao' is the universal source of being that transcends the dichotomy of subjective and objective. Even the modern iterations leading to Schopenhauer and Nietzsche credit the mind with a unique role in 'self-overcoming'.

James Allen's *As a Man Thinketh* expands upon that tradition. Indeed, the name of the work comes from the Book of Proverbs chapter 23, verse 7: 'As a man thinketh in his heart, so is he.' *As a Man Thinketh* takes the proposition further by considering exactly how it is that mind is able to act on the material plane.

The book starts with a big, bold statement: that men and women 'are themselves makers of themselves'. Nevertheless, it adds, we are usually more anxious to improve our circumstances rather than ourselves. This is why we remain trapped. We would do better to engage the universe's 'hidden justice'—namely, that whenever a man applies himself to remedy his character, he begins to make progress in life, the extent of the progress being in exact proportion to his altered mental condition.

That is done, says Allen, by ensuring that the thoughts, visions, and ideals held in the mind are consistent with those of the person we wish to become. Such visions are realized by way of an inexorable logic: thought crystallizes into habit and habit solidifies into circumstance. It is worth taking note of two subtleties of Allen's thinking here. First, it is your *sustained* vision that is manifested, not your idle whims and wishes. And second, *all* thoughts—not only desirable and productive ones—are capable of being realized in actuality. 'Every thought-seed sown or allowed to fall into the mind and to take root there,' says Allen, 'produces its own, blossoming sooner or later into act, and bearing its own fruitage of opportunity and circumstances.'

Ultimately, the best course is to sustain the mental intention necessary to actually *become* the person who will be able to give effect to it. Men do not attract that which they *want*, but that which they *are*. If you want to lead, you must work to *be* a man whose qualities inspire others to follow. If you want to prosper, you must work to *be* a man capable of providing the value that others will requite with value of their own. If you want to entertain and charm, you must work to *be* a man who is engaging, gracious, and responsive. The kind of thought necessary to engage these processes is one that is directed at remedying the cause, which invariably is found in some aspect of ourselves.

For the modern man, there is nothing more empowering than being reminded that our nature and prospects really are of our own making. The poet William Blake once wrote how he would hear in the voices of his fellow Londoners what he called 'mind-forg'd manacles'—the mental restraints and limitations imposed by themselves and others on the natural potential of their being. *As a Man Thinketh* provides a key to unlock those manacles and loosen those bonds. Ask first: *What do I wish to achieve?* And then: *What person am I to become in order to achieve it?*

As a Man Thinketh

EFFECT OF THOUGHT ON CIRCUMSTANCES

Man's mind may be likened to a garden, which may be intelligently cultivated or allowed to run wild; but whether cultivated or neglected, it must, and will, *bring forth*. If no useful seeds are *put* into it, then an abundance of useless weed-seeds will *fall* therein, and will continue to produce their kind.

Just as a gardener cultivates his plot, keeping it free from weeds, and growing the flowers and fruits which he requires, so may a man tend the garden of his mind, weeding out all the wrong, useless, and impure thoughts, and cultivating toward perfection the flowers and fruits of right, useful, and pure thoughts. By pursuing this process, a man sooner or later discovers that he is the master-gardener of his soul, the director of his life. He also reveals, within himself, the laws of thought, and understands, with ever-increasing accuracy, how the thought-forces and mind elements operate in the shaping of his character, circumstances, and destiny.

Thought and character are one, and as character can only manifest and discover itself through environment and circumstance, the outer conditions of a person's life will always be found to be harmoniously related to his inner state. This does not mean that a man's circumstances at any given time are an indication of his *entire* character, but that those circumstances are so intimately connected with some vital thought-element within himself that, for the time being, they are indispensable to his development.

Every man is where he is by the law of his being; the thoughts which he has built into his character have brought him there, and in the arrangement of his life there is no element of chance, but all is the result of a law which cannot err. This is just as true of those who feel 'out of harmony' with their surroundings as of those who are contented with them.

As a progressive and evolving being, man is where he is that he may learn that he may grow; and as he learns the spiritual lesson which any circumstance contains for him, it passes away and gives place to other circumstances.

Man is buffeted by circumstances so long as he believes himself to be the creature of outside conditions, but when he realizes that he is a creative power, and that he may command the hidden soil and seeds of his being out of which circumstances grow, he then becomes the rightful master of himself.

That circumstances grow out of thought every man knows who has for any length of time practised self-control and self-purification, for he will have noticed that the alteration in his circumstances has been in exact ratio with his altered mental condition. So true is this that when a man earnestly applies himself to remedy the defects in his character, and makes swift and marked progress, he passes rapidly through a succession of vicissitudes.

The soul attracts that which it secretly harbours; that which it loves, and also that which it fears; it reaches the height of its cherished aspirations; it falls to the level of its unchastened desires—and circumstances are the means by which the soul receives its own.

Every thought-seed sown or allowed to fall into the mind, and to take root there, produces its own, blossoming sooner or later into act, and bearing its own fruitage of opportunity and circumstance. Good thoughts bear good fruit, bad thoughts bad fruit.

The outer world of circumstance shapes itself to the inner world of thought, and both pleasant and unpleasant external conditions are factors, which make for the ultimate good of the individual. As the reaper of his own harvest, man learns both by suffering and bliss.

Following the inmost desires, aspirations, thoughts, by which he allows himself to be dominated, pursuing the will-o'-the-wisps of impure imaginings or steadfastly walking the highway of strong and high endeavour, a man at last arrives at their fruition and fulfilment in the outer conditions of his life. The laws of growth and adjustment everywhere obtains.

A man does not come to the almshouse or the jail by the tyranny of fate or circumstance, but by the pathway of grovelling thoughts and base desires. Nor does a pure-minded man fall suddenly into crime by stress of any mere external force; the criminal thought had long been secretly fostered in the heart, and the hour of opportunity revealed its gathered power. Circumstance does not make the man; it reveals him to himself. No such conditions can exist as descending into vice and its attendant sufferings apart from vicious inclinations, or ascending into virtue and its pure happiness without the continued cultivation of virtuous aspirations; and man, therefore, as the lord and master of thought, is the maker of himself the shaper and author of environment. Even at birth the soul comes to its own and through every step of its earthly pilgrimage it attracts those combinations of conditions which reveal itself, which are the reflections of its own purity and, impurity, its strength and weakness.

Men do not attract that which they *want*, but that which they *are*. Their whims, fancies, and ambitions are thwarted at every step, but their inmost thoughts and desires are fed with their own food, be it foul or clean. The 'divinity that shapes our ends' is in ourselves; it is our very self. Only himself manacles man: thought and action are the gaolers of Fate—they imprison, being base; they are also the angels of Freedom—they liberate, being noble. Not what he wishes and prays for does a man get, but what he justly earns. His wishes and prayers are only gratified and answered when they harmonize with his thoughts and actions.

In the light of this truth, what, then, is the meaning of 'fighting against circumstances?' It means that a man is continually revolting against an *effect* without, while all the time he is nourishing and preserving its *cause* in his heart. That cause may take the form of a conscious vice or an unconscious weakness; but whatever it is, it stubbornly retards the efforts of its possessor, and thus calls aloud for remedy.

Men are anxious to improve their circumstances, but are unwilling to improve themselves; they therefore remain bound. The man who does not shrink from self-crucifixion can never fail to accomplish the object upon which his heart is set. This is as true of earthly as of heavenly things. Even the man whose sole object is to acquire wealth must be prepared to make great personal sacrifices before he can accomplish his object; and how much more so he who would realize a strong and well-poised life?

Here is a man who is wretchedly poor. He is extremely anxious that his surroundings and home comforts should be improved, yet all the time he shirks his work, and considers he is justified in trying to deceive his employer on the ground of the insufficiency of his wages. Such a man does not understand the simplest rudiments of those principles which are the basis of true prosperity, and is not only totally unfitted to rise out of his wretchedness, but is actually attracting to himself a still deeper wretchedness by dwelling in, and acting out, indolent, deceptive, and unmanly thoughts.

Here is a rich man who is the victim of a painful and persistent disease as the result of gluttony. He is willing to give large sums of money to get rid of it, but he will not sacrifice his gluttonous desires. He wants to gratify his taste for rich and unnatural viands and have his health as well. Such a man is totally unfit to have health, because he has not yet learned the first principles of a healthy life.

Here is an employer of labour who adopts crooked measures to avoid paying the regulation wage, and, in the hope of making larger profits, reduces the wages of his workpeople. Such a man is altogether unfitted for prosperity, and when he finds himself bankrupt, both as regards reputation and riches, he blames circumstances, not knowing that he is the sole author of his condition.

I have introduced these three cases merely as illustrative of the truth that man is the causer (though nearly always unconsciously) of his circumstances, and that, whilst aiming at a good end, he is continually frustrating its accomplishment by encouraging thoughts and desires which cannot possibly harmonize with that end. Such cases could be multiplied and varied almost indefinitely, but this is not necessary, as the reader can, if he so resolves, trace the action of the laws of thought in his own mind and life, and until this is done, mere external facts cannot serve as a ground of reasoning.

Circumstances, however, are so complicated, thought is so deeply rooted, and the conditions of happiness vary so vastly with individuals, that a man's entire soul-condition (although it may be known to himself) cannot be judged by another from the external aspect of his life alone. A man may be honest in certain directions, yet suffer privations; a man may be dishonest in certain directions, yet acquire wealth; but the conclusion usually formed that the one man fails *because of his particular honesty,* and that the other *prospers because of his particular dishonesty,* is the result of a superficial judgment, which assumes that the dishonest man is almost totally corrupt, and the honest man almost entirely virtuous. In the light of a deeper knowledge and wider experience such judgment is found to be erroneous. The dishonest man may have some admirable virtues, which the other does, not possess; and the honest man obnoxious vices which are absent in the other. The honest man reaps the good results of his honest thoughts and acts; he also brings upon himself the sufferings, which his vices produce. The dishonest man likewise garners his own suffering and happiness.

It is pleasing to human vanity to believe that one suffers because of one's virtue; but not until a man has extirpated every sickly, bitter, and impure thought from his mind, and washed every sinful stain from his soul, can he be in a position to know and declare that his sufferings are the result of his good, and not of his bad qualities; and on the way to, yet long before he has reached, that supreme perfection, he will have found, working in his mind and life, the Great Law which is absolutely just, and which cannot, therefore, give good for evil, evil for good. Possessed of such knowledge, he will then know, looking back upon his past ignorance and blindness, that his life is, and always was, justly ordered, and that all his past experiences, good and bad, were the equitable outworking of his evolving, yet unevolved self.

Good thoughts and actions can never produce bad results; bad thoughts and actions can never produce good results. This is but saying that nothing can come from corn but corn, nothing from nettles but nettles. Men understand this law in the natural world, and work with it; but few understand it in the mental and moral world (though its operation there is just as simple and undeviating), and they, therefore, do not co-operate with it.

Suffering is *always* the effect of wrong thought in some direction. It is an indication that the individual is out of harmony with himself, with the Law of his being. The sole and supreme use of suffering is to purify, to burn out all that is useless and impure. Suffering ceases for him who is pure. There could be no object in burning gold after the dross had been removed, and a perfectly pure and enlightened being could not suffer.

The circumstances which a man encounters with suffering are the result of his own mental inharmony. The circumstances which a man encounters with blessedness are the result of his own mental harmony.

Blessedness, not material possessions, is the measure of right thought; wretchedness, not lack of material possessions, is the measure of wrong thought. A man may be cursed and rich; he may be blessed and poor. Blessedness and riches are only joined together when the riches are rightly and wisely used; and the poor man only descends into wretchedness when he regards his lot as a burden unjustly imposed.

Indigence and indulgence are the two extremes of wretchedness. They are both equally unnatural and the result of mental disorder. A man is not rightly conditioned until he is a happy, healthy, and prosperous being; and happiness, health, and prosperity are the result of a harmonious adjustment of the inner with the outer, of the man with his surroundings.

A man only begins to be a man when he ceases to whine and revile, and commences to search for the hidden justice which regulates his life. And as he adapts his mind to that regulating factor, he ceases to accuse others as the cause of his condition, and builds himself up in strong and noble thoughts; ceases to kick against circumstances, but begins to *use* them as aids to his more rapid progress, and as a means of discovering the hidden powers and possibilities within himself.

Law, not confusion, is the dominating principle in the universe; justice, not injustice, is the soul and substance of life; and righteousness, not corruption, is the moulding and moving force in the spiritual government of the world. This being so, man has but to right himself to find that the universe is right; and during the process of putting himself right he will find that as he alters his thoughts towards things and other people, things and other people will alter towards him.

The proof of this truth is in every person, and it therefore admits of easy investigation by systematic introspection and self-analysis. Let a man radically alter his thoughts, and he will be astonished at the rapid transformation it will effect in the material conditions of his life. Men imagine that thought can be kept secret, but it cannot; it rapidly crystallizes into habit, and habit solidifies into circumstance. Bestial thoughts crystallize into habits of drunkenness and sensuality, which solidify into circumstances of destitution and disease; impure thoughts of every kind crystallize into enervating and confusing habits, which solidify into distracting and adverse circumstances; thoughts of fear, doubt, and indecision crystallize into weak, unmanly, and irresolute habits, which solidify into circumstances of failure, indigence, and slavish dependence; lazy thoughts crystallize into habits of uncleanliness and dishonesty, which solidify into circumstances of foulness and beggary; hateful and condemnatory thoughts crystallize into habits of accusation and violence, which solidify into circumstances of injury and persecution; selfish thoughts of all kinds crystallize into habits of self-seeking, which solidify into circumstances more or less distressing. On the other hand, beautiful thoughts of all kinds crystallize into habits of grace and kindliness, which solidify into genial and sunny circumstances; pure thoughts crystallize into habits of temperance and self-control, which solidify into circumstances of repose and peace; thoughts of courage, self-reliance, and decision crystallize into manly habits, which solidify into circumstances of success, plenty, and freedom; energetic thoughts crystallize into habits of cleanliness and industry, which solidify into circumstances of pleasantness; gentle and forgiving thoughts crystallize into habits of gentleness, which solidify into protective and preservative circumstances; loving and unselfish thoughts crystallize into habits of self-forgetfulness for others, which solidify into circumstances of sure and abiding prosperity and true riches.

A particular train of thought persisted in, be it good or bad, cannot fail to produce its results on the character and circumstances. A man cannot *directly* choose his circumstances, but he can choose his thoughts, and so indirectly, yet surely, shape his circumstances.

Nature helps every man to the gratification of the thoughts, which he most encourages, and opportunities are presented which will most speedily bring to the surface both the good and evil thoughts.

Let a man cease from his sinful thoughts, and all the world will soften towards him, and be ready to help him; let him put away his weakly and sickly thoughts, and lo, opportunities will spring up on every hand to aid his strong resolves; let him encourage good thoughts, and no hard fate shall bind him down to wretchedness and shame. The world is your kaleidoscope, and the varying combinations of colours, which at every succeeding moment it presents to you are the exquisitely adjusted pictures of your ever-moving thoughts.

'So you will be what you will to be;
Let failure find its false content
In that poor word, 'environment',
But spirit scorns it, and is free.

'It masters time, it conquers space;
It cowes that boastful trickster, Chance,
And bids the tyrant Circumstance
Uncrown, and fill a servant's place.

'The human Will, that force unseen,
The offspring of a deathless Soul,
Can hew a way to any goal,
Though walls of granite intervene.

'Be not impatient in delays
But wait as one who understands;
When spirit rises and commands
The gods are ready to obey.'

211

CONCLUSION

The existence of what is known as the 'perennial philosophy'—the universal core of spiritual wisdom that is found in multiple traditions—has been long known. Where this book is unique is in identifying the spiritual classics arising out of that tradition that retain the power to transform lives. It is intended to be a vehicle for communicating insight and inspiration from the most profound of our forebears in a way that is fresh, engaging, and relevant to the general reader today.

What insights are at the heart of these works?

Time and time again the spiritual classics refer to a *unifying force* or principle that lies behind the apparent multiplicity we encounter in the world. To a greater or lesser degree, we humans are inseparably connected to this force and have recourse to its power and energy, in particular when we are able to tame the distractions of the egoic 'monkey mind' and access the higher self.

The spiritual classics also refer repeatedly to the quality of *detachment*. The *Bhagavad Gita*, famously, has advised us that we must take action in the world, while at the same time renouncing the 'fruits of action'. The Buddhist and Daoist traditions promote a similar view, the former telling us that suffering arises as a result of attachment and that liberation is attained when attachment ceases, and the latter speaking of the benefits of 'actionless action'. When we do act, it is essential that we act first to change ourselves, rather than the world, since the world is infinitely responsive and it is the qualities of each individual that will determine their reality.

The spiritual classics likewise take a relatively consistent approach to the question of *causality*. This causality can operate on the physical plane: our every act will have consequences, whether those consequences occur in the immediate present, or whether they manifest many years, decades, or even centuries in the future. This causality can, equally, operate from the mental to the physical plane: our every 'thought-seed' blossoms sooner or later into an act which then has the capacity to set in course a chain of causes and effects in the material world. The fact that we cannot perceive the full extent of this network of causes and effects—a fact that is recognized in so many of the spiritual classics—is neither here nor there. Truth, as Rumi has told us, is like an elephant in a dark room, whose totality we can never fully grasp.

There remains one final question: In the light of what the great spiritual masters have communicated in these works, what kind of person should we aim to become?

Time and again the works hark back to a basic principle: *be your own point of origin*. This means to act proactively not reactively. It means to become an 'uncaused' cause. It means to stand at the calm centre of the storm, able to act outwardly while remaining inwardly unaffected. This is the time-tested path transmuting the reactive lower aspects of humanity into a higher self that is closer in nature to the original source of being.

This poses a challenge: to become your own point of origin means to no longer be a 'subject'. It means to adopt a mode of being opposed to those who rely upon subjection to prosper and who prefer men to live in the reactive state, buffeted to and fro by impulses that can readily be manipulated by way of mass education, the mainstream media, social conformity, or other environmental pressures and cues. A man in the reactive state, even when he thinks he is thinking, feeling, or acting on his own account and on his own behalf, is a man with buttons to be pushed and triggers pulled. A man who becomes his own point of origin, on the other hand, is a man on the point of breaking through his conditioning and becoming a force for *real* change in the world.

The spiritual classics in this book have never suggested that the path will be easy. Quite the contrary: to reach the 'unconditioned' state requires nothing less than the controlled demolition and gradual rebuilding of the self. But there has never been a better time—or a more important period in history—at which to make a start.

Bibliography

Al-Ghazali. *The Alchemy of Happiness*. Translated by Claud Field. London: John Murray, 1910.

Allen, James. *As a Man Thinketh*. New York: 1903.

Chuang-tzu. *Chuang Tzu: Mystic, Moralist, and Social Reformer*. Translated by Herbert Giles. London: Bernard Quaritch, 1889.

The Dhammapada: A Collection of Verses. Translated by F. Max Müller. Oxford: Clarendon Press, 1881.

Nietzsche, Friedrich. *Thus Spake Zarathustra*. Translated by Thomas Common. New York: The Modern Library, 1892.

Pascal, Blaise. *The Thoughts of Blaise Pascal*. Translated by C. Kegan Paul. London: George Bell & Sons, 1905.

Rumi, Jalaluddin. *The Teachings of Rumi: The Masnavi*. Translated by E.H. Whinfield. New York: E.P. Dutton & Co, 1975.

The Sacred Books of China: The Texts of Taoism. Translated by James Legge. Oxford: Clarendon Press, 1891.

The Sacred Books of the East Vol. VIII: Bhagavadgita, Sanatsugatiya, Anugita. Translated by F. Max Müller. 2nd ed. Oxford: Clarendon Press, 1898.

Schopenhauer, Arthur. *Essays of Arthur Schopenhauer.* Translated by T. Bailey Saunders. New York: A.L. Burt Company, 1902.

The World English Bible (WEB).

Three Initiates. *The Kybalion.* Chicago: Yogi Publication Society, 1908.

ALSO AVAILABLE

CLASSIC PHILOSOPHY FOR THE MODERN MAN

ANDREW LYNN

'What you hold in your hands is a handbook for living: it is an account of how the greatest minds have spoken to us on how to grow and prosper as flesh-and-blood human beings.'

Classic Philosophy for the Modern Man is inspired by a single concept: that, to thrive in the world, we need ready access to the practical wisdom of our forebears. It answers that need by introducing for the general reader the most powerful and enduringly relevant works of great thinkers from around the world. Together these works teach us how to achieve excellence; how to obtain and exercise power, advance in the world, and live gracefully; how to cultivate nobility of soul; and – above all – how to be one's own man. There is no better primer in the art of living well.

219

Generativity

Andrew Lynn

We are all in search of answers to the mystery of human achievement. Why do some people excel while others do not?

In answering that question, *Generativity* will take you on a journey from the ancient Zoroastrians and the secret gospels of Nag Hammadi to the most recent scientific insights on expertise and peak performance.

Tracing the stories of outstanding individuals in the light of both traditional wisdom and modern science, Andrew Lynn examines the universal source of superior achievement in athletics, art, science, music, scholarship, politics, and business. *Generativity* is a uniquely accessible and wide-ranging account of what it is that makes us exceptional.

Made in the USA
San Bernardino, CA
27 September 2018